THE SECRET LIFE OF GRIEF

ALSO BY TANJA PAJEVIC

9 Steps to Heal Your Resentment and Reboot Your Marriage

THE SECRET LIFE OF GRIEF

A Memoir

Tanja Pajevic

Abbondanza Press

Boulder, CO

Abbondanza Press

© 2016 by Tanja Pajevic

Published in the United States by Abbondanza Press.
ISBN 978-0-9863031-3-5 (paperback)
ISBN 978-0-9863031-2-8 (eBook)

Cover design by Thomas McGee at Rightly Designed.
Interior design by Hynek Palatin.

First edition (Version 1.1)

DISCLAIMER

This is a work of creative nonfiction. I have recreated events and conversations from my notes and journals, portraying them to the best of my knowledge. Any mistakes or inaccuracies are mine. I have changed the names of most but not all of the individuals in this book, and in some cases I also modified identifying details in order to preserve anonymity.

For Nico, Gabriel, Ken
and my mama.

There must be those among whom we can sit down and weep,
and still be counted as warriors.

—ADRIENNE RICH,
SOURCES

CONTENTS

INTRODUCTION

In the United States, we don't talk about grief. After the memorial or funeral, our coworkers, neighbors and friends expect us to get back to our lives, as if nothing happened. As if we haven't been forever changed.

We no longer have a socially accepted model for grieving in the U.S., and it shows. Instead of wearing mourning black and seeing our loss reflected in our community, we mourn at home, cut off and alone. As a result, most of us have no idea how to grieve. We stuff down our feelings and pretend we're fine. All while wondering where to turn, wishing we had support.

When my father died in 1993, the unresolved grief I felt around his death cost me nearly a decade as I struggled to make sense of what had happened and how to recover. I didn't want to make that same mistake when my mother died in 2012. This time around, I wanted to grieve consciously.

But how?

After polling friends and acquaintances for tips—and receiving the usual "time heals all wounds" and "the first year is the hardest"—I turned to books. Surely, someone had figured this out, could show me what to *do* with my grief. How to survive.

What I found instead were stacks of memoirs devoted to the dying process. I'd already walked my mother to death's door, though, and wanted help in navigating what came next. What happened *after* the funeral, once everyone went home?

Furthermore, I wanted reassurance that my grief was a normal and healthy emotion. That there wasn't something wrong with me for feeling my loss so deeply. And I wanted to read about someone who'd not only survived that first year, but who'd done so with laughter, even. Grace.

The Secret Life of Grief picks up where those other memoirs leave off. It explores what grief and mourning mean in a culture that pretends death doesn't exist, within a medical model that believes we can cheat death at all costs.

This is a book for those of us who aren't willing to "pull it together" and act like nothing's wrong. Who can't—or won't—stuff our feelings, and who recognize that grief and mourning are a normal part of life, a deep and healthy human emotion.

At its heart, *The Secret Life of Grief* is a book for those of us who believe in the transformative power of loss. And it's a book for those of us who believe in love.

In the three years since my mother died, I've learned that there is no "right" way to do grief. There is no *one* answer when it comes to grief, no "one-size-fits-all."

Our grief is as unique as we are, and just as essential to our lives as our laughter, love, hugs and tears. The people we love and the loss of those people, after all, make us who we are. They form the stories we share with each other late at night or early in the morning, over a cup of coffee or a glass of wine.

When we can share those stories with each other, we feel less alone. A good story can help illuminate even the darkest path.

This, then, is my story. Like every other tale of love, loss and redemption, it's messy and imperfect.

Grief is, too.

Therein lie its riches.

Tanja Pajevic

February 23, 2016

Boulder, CO

BOOK 1

GRACE

There are only two ways to live your life. One is as if nothing is a miracle. The other is as though everything is a miracle.

—ALBERT EINSTEIN

CHAPTER 1

ALPENGLOW

My mother died at dawn, as magnificent pink streaks spread across a blackened sky. I was asleep in the bottom bunk of my four-year-old's bed when a deep sense of peace awoke me. Hazy light shone through the curtain. I sighed deeply before being pulled back under.

A few minutes later, my brother Marko called to tell me she'd passed. The preceding few months had been brutal and beautiful, and now that my mother had died, I possessed a sharp, new clarity. An aching, expanding silence filled within me. I rose, turned to tuck in my son, and kissed him, my hand on his round, innocent cheek. Then I went and dressed.

Ken heard me stirring. After a long hug, we addressed logistics. He would take the day off of work and stay with the children. Then he would call the nurse who was supposed to come today. What would he tell her? That we no longer needed her. My mother had just died.

Ken pressed a cup of coffee into my hand and I went out into this new world, alone. The sun was rising over the horizon as

I drove the short distance to my mother's condominium. When I arrived, I crawled into bed with her and hugged her tight. Then I laid my head on her shoulder, and sobbed like a young child.

I stayed like that for a long time, holding my mother, not wanting to let her go. My mother hadn't been physically demonstrative in life, and because of this, I clung to her now. I apologized for everything I'd messed up during her short, intense illness, for everything I hadn't had the courage to do or say. I told her how thankful I was that we'd spent the past decade in the same town, how blessed I was to have witnessed the deep bond between her and my children.

And I held on tight, my tears soaking her hospital gown. Yes, my mother was no longer suffering; yes, she'd finally found the peace I'd prayed for these last few weeks. All of this helped, but none of it dented the enormity of what had just happened. *I'd just lost my mother.*

The grief came in waves, easing up before taking me under again. Here and there, I'd get up and wander the condo before returning to my mother's side to smooth down her hair or hold her hand. In between, Marko and I would share some surreal observation about the hospice furniture crowding my mother's living room. When we'd brought her home from the hospital the night before, we thought she'd live for another week or two. Neither of us expected just one more night.

Sharp winter sun cut through the window, slicing through the cold December morning. Marko had chosen Vivaldi's *Four Seasons* to ease my mother's transition, and "Winter" was playing at full steam, the music brilliant to excess against our fresh, new loss.

My tears felt almost violent, erupting in the middle of a sentence, in the middle of a thought. In between my tears, I marveled over this sharpened clarity. I'd spent the past few months terrified of this moment. Here it was, finally, and I'd survived.

And not only had I survived, but I'd grown stronger, clearer in what mattered and what didn't. Taking care of my mother during her short, agonizing journey with cancer had taught me that death is just another part of life, as intense and as beautiful as birth. Walking my mother to death's door had taught me the power of redemption, the strength of forgiveness and the sheer beauty of love.

I was so incredibly thankful that I hadn't run or hidden during my mother's illness. Watching her die had been a crash course in how to live my life: all I'd had to do was be present, and keep my heart open. In return, I'd learned that life isn't meant to be an uphill struggle; that drama, ultimately, is worthless; and that despite everything mainstream religion teaches us, guilt isn't supposed to guide us—love is.

But the biggest waste of time was getting caught in the past or worrying about the future. As long as we could stay in the present moment, life gave us exactly what we needed. And yet so many of us missed this by ruminating about the past or worrying about what *might* happen, as if that would somehow lessen the pain when tragedy struck. But the only thing worrying does is rob us of the time we have left. And we can never, ever get that back.

At some point, I went into my mother's bedroom, opened her jewelry box and put on her wedding rings. My parents' union hadn't been an easy one; after 17 years together, they'd bitterly divorced. Shortly thereafter, as my father's tool and die machine shop was going bankrupt, he was diagnosed with colon cancer. He died a year and a half later, months after I graduated from college—sending me into a downward spiral that darkened my 20s as I tried to come to terms with my broken relationship with my father.

But now, none of that mattered. For perhaps the first time, I was deeply, intensely grateful to both of my parents. Whatever else had happened, I was here because of them. *My children* were here because of them.

It seemed incredibly important to honor that union—a problematic one, yes, but one characterized by love and happiness, however briefly. Putting on those rings was a way of completing the circle that would forever be known as my first family, of honoring the profound knowledge that both of my parents were now dead.

I moved the rings to another finger, and sat down on my mother's bed. Whatever had happened between my parents in this lifetime was at rest. I could feel it. It had taken well over 20 years, but they were both finally free.

As was I. Free to step away from the pain of the old stories, free to see my parents' marriage for what it was: a sacred union that had simply outlived its time.

In late September of 2012, my mother went in for a round of pre-surgery testing before undergoing hip replacement surgery. The tests came back clean, and my mother was given the green light for surgery. At age 73, my mother was still the strong-willed, independent woman she'd always been, ready to resume the more active lifestyle she'd enjoyed before the hip she'd broken the previous fall refused to heal.

Before she underwent that surgery, my mother scheduled a last-minute colonoscopy to address some stomach issues that had been bothering her for a few months. But she wasn't able to drink the pre-surgery laxative prep without vomiting, so her gastrointestinal (GI) doctor did an upper scope instead. After finding evidence of H. pylori in her stomach, he sent her home with an antibiotic. The antibiotics, however, just made everything worse, and it wasn't long before she was unable to keep down any food. When my mother called the doctors for help, they brushed her off. It's just the medicine, they told her. Keep at it.

Two weeks later, I brought my mother to the emergency room so they could treat her for dehydration. The doctors admitted her to the hospital and started all sorts of tests to figure out what was causing her vomiting. CT scans, X-rays, blood tests—everything came back clean. And still, she couldn't keep any food down.

After the first two days, her GI doctor, Pugliese, pulled a specialist in on my mother's case, but he wasn't able to pinpoint the source of her symptoms, either. On the third day, they decided to go ahead with the colonoscopy in hopes of finding an answer.

The procedure was scheduled for noon on Friday, October 12, making my mother grumpy because it was right in the middle of her soaps. At least the procedure would be quick, she said; with any luck, she'd be back in her room in time for *General Hospital*.

By 1:15 p.m., I was sitting in my mother's hospital room with Marko, waiting. While he worked, I closed my eyes and sent my mom strong, healing thoughts. I'd never done anything like that before, but I felt she needed it.

An hour later, Dr. Pugliese appeared in the doorway, followed by a surgeon we'd never met. They'd found cancer in my mother's abdomen, he said. They weren't sure where it had started, but it had already spread to her colon, and was probably the cause of her symptoms. In fact, her colon was so weak that he'd inadvertently punctured it, and now this Dr. Hudson was going to perform emergency surgery to repair it.

The surgeon stepped forward—tall, thin, handsome, everything Pugliese was not—explained briefly what would happen, then handed us a bunch of release forms.

I looked at them in shock, feeling weird and light-headed, as if time had stopped. Marko took over and fired off a bunch of questions.

"We're not sure how far the cancer's spread," Hudson said. "It appears to be a rare, advanced form, but we'll be able to tell you more after the tests come back. "Right now, we can't do anything until we get in there and repair your mother's colon. She's septic. There's no time to waste."

Marko grabbed the pen and signed. "But she'll be OK," he said, "right?"

Hudson looked us in the eye. "I don't know."

My legs started to shake, moving from the adrenaline.

"We'll do the best we can," he said as he left.

The pale, bloated GI doctor stayed behind. Pugliese apologized again, profusely. He wasn't sure if he'd punctured the colon, he said, or if it had simply been so weak that it had broken from the pressure.

Pugliese paused, waiting for our reaction, and in that endless moment, I felt as if I could see right through him. He might have been in his mid-50s, but all I saw before me was a scared little boy, a fuck-up who'd always wanted to please his parents, but had never gotten it right.

And now he wanted our absolution.

Pugliese rambled on, assuring us what a great surgeon Hudson was, joking how everyone who'd been scheduled for surgery had to wait since my mother had been pushed to the front of the line.

All I could do was look at him, in horror. The anger was kicking in now, mixing with adrenaline, and I wanted to smash his sorry little face into the ground.

Two hours later, my mother was in the intensive care unit (ICU), fighting for her life. When they finally let us in to see her, a dour-looking doctor told us how five of my mother's major organs had shut down, including her lungs and kidneys; how the only reason her heart was still beating was from the drugs they were pumping into her system; how she'd gone septic, so septic she only had a 10% chance of surviving the night. And by the way, she was so full of cancer that she probably didn't have long to live—assuming that she survived the night, that is.

Pause. Which was a pretty big assumption.

I stared at him in shock, my head oddly disconnected from my body. I found myself looking at my hands while he talked, fingernails I'd recently polished gold because it was something small I could do for myself, something *fun*. At some point, I realized I was shaking. My arms were moving by themselves, as were my legs. I kicked them instinctively, desperately wanting to run.

Once I pulled myself together, I called Ken to bring in Nico and Gabriel, our six- and four-year-old children, to say goodbye to my mother. They'd brought along artwork they'd made for her, and as I watched my children tape get-well cards to her bed, I thought: a four-year-old should not be seeing this. And: how can he *not* be seeing this?

I spent the rest of the night by my mother's bedside, bargaining with God. I didn't care about the cancer; all I wanted was a few more days or weeks to say goodbye. But for that to happen, my mother had to make it through the night, and for that to happen, she had to make it through the next hour.

In between those prayers, I prayed to my mother. *Borrow my strength*, I said silently. *Take whatever you need.* Over and over again, like a mantra.

Each hour my mother stayed alive increased her chances for recovery. Three ICU nurses took over where the attending doc had left off, and I watched intently as they followed protocol, inserting a seemingly endless array of medicines into the lines snaking out from her body. After a while, we settled into an uneasy silence, with me sitting next to my mother's bed, holding her hand, while the nurses worked to save her life.

Slowly, steadily, miracles began to happen. When a surgical team couldn't be found to insert a critical port into my mother's heart to deliver more life-saving meds, one of the nurses suggested an experimental leg port—something none of the other nurses had ever attempted. It worked.

Another gift came from the sheer number of nurses at my mother's disposal. While the ICU nurses normally cared for

three patients at once, tonight had been quiet, freeing up a second nurse to help my mother. The third nurse—the only one
experienced in inserting the leg port—wasn't even supposed to
be working, and was only in the ward because of a scheduling
mix-up.

I learned all this from my mother's primary nurse, Carla.
"But what would have happened if that extra nurse hadn't been
here?" I asked. "Would you have still done the leg port?"

She shook her head. "No, I've never done it before."

"The other nurse?"

"None of us have ever done it before."

"Then what would have happened?"

Carla paused. "Your mother needed that port. It's a good
thing we got it in when we did."

I sat back in my seat, swirling in a sort of thankful shock.
This was how the hours passed, full and intense as hell. The
clock continued to inch forward, each hour giving rise to that
much more hope, that much more *life*. My mother had been
admitted into the ICU in the early afternoon; by 11:00 p.m.,
we were down to two nurses. By 1:00 a.m., we were down to
one.

Somewhere in the pre-dawn hush, I fell asleep in a chair
next to my mother's bed. I awoke to hear her telling me she was
going to be sick, that she needed help. I ran to get Carla, and a
second nurse jumped in, increasing her anti-nausea medication
and stabilizing her other meds.

Then I remembered that my mother had a breathing tube in
her mouth.

I looked at Carla, who was adjusting more lines. "I thought
you said she couldn't talk."

She looked up. "She can't."

"But I heard her. I'm sure of it."

Carla didn't say anything, just looked at me, and I couldn't shake the feeling that she'd encountered miracles like this before, if not on a regular basis.

By morning, my mother was conscious, alert but heavily drugged. When the dour-faced ICU doctor appeared for his rounds, he was surprised to find my mother still alive.

"How did you get to be so tough," he asked. "Do you eat nails for breakfast?"

Later, he apologized, saying he hadn't meant to be unnecessarily harsh. He'd simply wanted us to realize the severity of the situation, to prepare us for the very real chance that my mother could easily have died.

I looked at him, but said nothing. I could forgive him, or I could maintain my anger—right now, it was too much to decide. Besides, he was just the doctor who'd happened to be on duty. As far as I was concerned, it was the nurses who'd saved my mother's life.

And yet, we weren't anywhere close to being out of the woods. My mother had survived the first night, but there were all sorts of milestones that needed to still happen, from breathing on her own to stabilizing her blood pressure to moving her out of the ICU. Then there would be another two weeks in the cardiac unit followed by another three in rehab while we tried to get my mother strong enough to bring her home.

Throughout it all, we wrestled with the knowledge that a rare, advanced form of appendiceal cancer was growing in her abdomen. Without chemo, the doctors told her, she had another three to six months to live.

Two months later, my mother was dead.

My anger is immense, a moving target. It falls on anyone who happens to be in my way: family, friends, strangers. At first, it's directed at the oncologists who couldn't give us a straight answer during the last two weeks of my mother's life, as Marko and I were struggling to understand what was happening and trying to decide whether or not to bring my mother home from the hospital. My mother had wanted to die at home, and Marko and I were incensed that we'd been cheated out of those precious, final days because her doctors hadn't had the courage to tell us she was dying.

I write it all down, penning long missives to the docs about their terrible bedside manner, telling them how important it is that they get their profession together. Stop acting like assholes, I write, and start acting like you're human. Remember that your patients are more than the sum of their charts—they're people, too, with loved ones, just like you. Elisabeth Kübler-Ross can only do so much, I write; it's time for you to get your shit together. I title it "First, Do No Harm."

Before long, my wrath turns to Jeremy, an old family friend who hadn't been able to reach out to my mother as she was dying. Over the years, Jeremy and my mother had a loving but troubled relationship, and now I'm beyond pissed that he hadn't contacted her as she was dying. Meanwhile, he's asked Marko if he can join us for the services. I do not, will not allow it.

My fury rages, unabated, for days. Throughout, Marko does his best to talk me down from my precarious ledge, offering me all sorts of compromises and outs. But I've become silly, over-rated, a caricature in a Doctor Seuss book, and I do not, *will not* budge.

After a while, Ken steps in. Then Marko again. Somewhere, in the back of my mind, I know I'm being unreasonable. And yet I won't give, *not one inch*. For the first time, I'm no longer willing to play peacemaker. I'm so fucking angry that I'm done, *do you hear me, done.*

Round and round we go. Unlike most of our friends, Marko and I don't have relatives in the U.S. besides our spouses and children; our parents emigrated from the former Yugoslavia, where the rest of our relatives still live. Meaning, we have no one else to pull into our bizarre little drama.

Which, in a twisted sort of way, makes my anger all the more relevant.

Of course, somewhere deep inside, a part of me realizes that my anger isn't simply about Jeremy. It's about the past, all those missed chances, everything we can never again repair.

It's also about the future. What I'll allow in my life from now on, and what I won't. After these last two god-awful months, I'm exhausted, tired from living my life in ways that don't make sense.

I'm tired of letting people get to me, tired of dealing with people who feel like they don't have my back. More than anything, then, my anger is a wall. It protects me.

I think of my mother as the late afternoon sun slides down the Rocky Mountain foothills in Boulder, CO, where I live. Afternoons were her favorite time of day, and she loved to spend this time with a cup of coffee, relaxing. In the hospital, she asked the nurses to help her into a chair by the window, where the afternoon sun shone down upon her.

I can't look at these mountains without thinking of my mother, without remembering how much time she spent staring at these foothills, knowing she was dying. After the oncologist gave her a few months to live, she spent as much time as she could by that damn hospital window, soaking up the late afternoon sun.

What was she thinking? How do you prepare to die?

In the first few weeks after her surgery, I'd ask my mother if she wanted to talk. But my mother had always been a private person, and I quickly learned that she wanted to be alone during these times, to sit in her own heavy silence.

Never mind that I was heartbroken by that silence, overcome with grief and the simple, awful knowledge that my mother was dying. As much as I wanted to, I couldn't ask her to be someone she wasn't, couldn't crack the shell that had always been her protection. My mother might only have had a few weeks left to live, but those were her weeks, not mine.

I think of all this—all this and more, depending on the day—when I see that late afternoon sun lighting up the foothills. There she is in the hospital, after that first surgery. There she is, lying on her couch at home. There she is, there she is, *there she is.*

At times, the memories come so sharply that they unearth me. My love for my mother comes coursing through, so deep and so pure that it almost knocks me over. If I'm not careful, this bright, intense feeling of love begins to cut as the sun slides behind the mountains, leaving me with a cold and painful melancholy.

On good days, I can weave my way through by letting the pain surface alongside the memories. Because life goes on, especially with young children at your side, reminding you to live.

On bad days, my children sustain me. They keep me plugged in and, for brief periods at a time, from falling into despair. Without them, I might very well crawl into bed and not come out.

But four-year-olds and six-year-olds are busy people, and I'm determined to remember the lessons I've learned about staying in the present moment. I don't try to hide my grief from my children, but I do temper it. I want them to know that it's fine to cry, but I don't want to overwhelm them with continual despair.

One afternoon, we visit the park beneath my mother's old hospital window. Despite the fact that the park is only a block away from the hospital, I've decided I won't let myself cry. So I motor on, determined not to succumb to the foothill's siren call. Determined—for once—to give my children a single, normal day without their mother breaking down before them. Minutes later, I'm sobbing behind my sunglasses, the stinging winter wind whipping my face as I push Gabriel higher on his swing, my heart breaking for something that no longer exists.

The following week, I take the children sledding at a park further north—far enough away from those damn foothills, I think, that I'll be safe. It's the season's first snowfall, and I want my children to have some good memories from this god-awful year. Minutes later, I'm crying silently behind my sunglasses as children scream and shout, sliding down the hill around me.

After this happens a few times, I no longer worry what the other parents will think; I simply focus on releasing the sobs before they overwhelm me. When my children ask why I'm sad, I answer honestly: I miss *Baba*, I say. I miss my mother, Milica.

But I'm here with my children, and I don't want to miss this moment, either. So I push through until I can feel something else break through the sadness—my two amazing children, their giant hearts so full of love.

After the local oncologists gave my mother three to six months to live, we took her to Denver to see a specialist—the only oncologist we could find who actually had any experience with her rare form of appendiceal cancer.

The university hospital was immense, bustling and chaotic, a Disneyland for cancer, replete with valet parking. Everywhere I looked, I saw people in various states of unrest: oxygen tubes, walkers, wheelchairs; every nook and cranny was crammed with patients and family members of varying makes and colors, toddlers as well as elders.

There, in the corner, stood a *Dazbog* coffee stand. I stopped and stared, struck by the symbolism. Russian and Serbian are both Slavic languages, similar enough that I can often make out a few words of Russian. I didn't know that *Dazbog* was the god of the sun and the rain, so I translated the word literally: "Give to me, God." Or, perhaps more appropriately, God giveth, and God taketh away.

Russian sayings lined the walls, and my mother stopped to try and sound out a few. The young woman behind the counter looked at my mother in surprise. She couldn't have been more than 20 years old, and I wondered what it must have been like to work in a place like this, surrounded by so many sick and dying.

My mother shook her head finally. "I don't know—I'm missing something."

Marko looked at the woman expectantly. "Well, what does it say?"

"No idea," the woman said. Her face was tight again, closed against the world. "I've no idea."

As my mother was dying, I found myself wanting a spiritual teacher. Not a therapist or church elder, but someone who'd already lost his or her mother and could help me navigate these scary waters.

Never mind that I'd lost my father 20 years before. Losing my mother was an entirely different animal, and I'd never felt more vulnerable or scared in my life. It didn't help that I had two young children at home who depended on me.

One day, a friend recommended David Harshada Wagner, a meditation teacher from the *Yogaglo* website. I scrolled through the site, amazed by the array of meditation videos he offered, from meditations for creativity to pre-game and pre-meeting meditations. I chose the meditation for grief and was sobbing in a matter of seconds, waves of grief shuddering through me.

Before long, I was doing at least one or two meditations every day. It was the only way I could function, survive the disparate worlds I now inhabited. If I could do a 15-minute meditation video after coming home from the hospital, I could pull myself together enough to put my kids to bed. Often, I sobbed my way through nearly the entire meditation.

I didn't know if this was right, but I didn't care. Because on the other side of those tears lived a much-needed sense of peace. And while that peace might have only lasted for a few minutes before the fear, anxiety and worry kicked back in, those minutes were everything.

On December 24th, seven days after my mother's death, I went out to buy my sister-in-law Leslie a birthday gift. It was the first time I'd been out on my own since my mother had died, and the first time I'd done anything unrelated to funeral planning.

I didn't have the courage to go to a mall, so I went to a small, local shop I thought I could get in and out of without incident. I realized my mistake as soon as I walked into the store. The store was bright, loud and chaotic; customers and saleswomen swirled about me, cheerful and chattering. Meanwhile, I functioned in a different dimension, my brain thickened and slowed, as if underwater.

And then—God help me—I ran into an acquaintance. For a few excruciating minutes, we made small talk. I have no idea what we said, just that I was trying to be something I was not— trying to be a woman who hadn't just lost her mother—and not completely freak out his son, who was standing between us.

I breathed with relief once they'd moved on and started circling the store again, looking for something for Leslie. But nothing felt right. Somehow, I'd convinced myself that finding the right gift was of supreme importance, almost as if by buying the correct gift, I could erase these past few months. Erase the fact that Leslie hadn't just lost her second mother.

I circled the store for what felt like hours, wondering how such a small decision could tie me into such knots. Finally, I held up two different pairs of earrings and asked a saleswoman for help.

Everything was fine until she told me how lucky I was to have a sister-in-law I got along with. And a brother in town, to boot!

"What about your parents," she asked. "Do they live here, too?"

The exterior of my body froze as every sluggish, dormant part of my insides surged to life. Surely, she could feel the electricity crackling off my skin, recognize the loss written all over my face.

For an eternal moment, I debated my answer. I could simply say, "No, my parents don't live here," but that was so obviously untrue that the words themselves might unhinge me as I spoke them.

Or I could say, "My father passed away a long time ago, and my mother just died." But that would put this woman on the spot, make her feel bad for asking.

For a split moment, that was *exactly* what I wanted—someone in this goddamn place to know that this wasn't Christmas for me, that we weren't all celebrating. My heart was broken in two, and here I was, about to pour my life story out to a complete stranger.

I couldn't do it. An excruciating amount of time had passed by now, but the saleswoman just stood there, looking at me expectantly. How was it possible that she didn't see me flayed open before her, grief coursing through me?

Finally, I choked down my words. "It's just us," I mumbled. "Just me and my brother."

In times of crisis, we drink coffee. In Yugoslavia, the country where my parents were born, good, strong coffee is a way of life, how you start your day as well as end it. An essential daily ritual, it's how you connect with friends and neighbors. In the Balkans, anything of importance happens in community.

When I was a child, we spent most of our summers visiting relatives in Yugoslavia. In 1975, when I was five years old, we spent the school year in Serbia in preparation for a permanent move back. But my parents aborted their plan at the last moment, and by the time we returned to Chicago, I'd forgotten English.

These days, Yugoslavia no longer exists. In the 1990s, after an intense series of wars and genocide fueled by century-old ethnic hatreds, the country broke apart into Slovenia, Croatia, Bosnia and Herzegovina, Serbia, Kosovo, Macedonia and Montenegro. Despite the resulting illness, joblessness and poverty, my relatives still congregate around coffee.

My mother was no exception. Even though she'd lived in the U.S. for over 40 years, she never lost her love for coffee. By the time I started drinking it as a teen, coffee had become one of the main ways my mother and I connected. Morning, afternoon, after-dinner; all that mattered was that it was good coffee, *strong* coffee.

Once I had my own family, that connection became even more deeply ingrained. With time at a premium as I tried to balance two young children with work, a husband and a dog, weekly afternoon coffees with my mother remained a shared ritual.

Good coffee bookmarked my mother's life to the end. During the last week of her life, barely able to eat or drink, much less speak, my mother was still asking for coffee. Starbucks, mind you. Not that watery stuff down the hall.

Now that she's gone, coffee's become that much more important—particularly the afternoon cup that was always such a highlight of her day.

These days, I drink that coffee alone. No matter how hard I try, I can't seem to talk Ken into joining me. *Are you sure?* I ask. *Not even half a cup? It's half-decaf!*

No thanks, he says. He wants to sleep tonight, not stay up from the caffeine.

What I don't say to him because I don't yet understand is that it's not about the coffee. It's my attempt to connect. To slow down the day and stop for a moment, honor who and what we are.

So I keep mixing and pouring, cooking and drinking. This: my afternoon. In my hand, a steaming cup of rich, redolent coffee.

My parents had been raised in an agrarian society and it showed; in the Chicago suburb where we lived, we stuck out like a sore thumb when my father spent weekends grilling bushels of red and green peppers my mother would then can. While our neighbors ate the canned and frozen meals of the day, we headed out to our garden for fresh vegetables or into the basement, where a leg of cured prosciutto hung above a giant vat of homemade yogurt.

If I wasn't already aware of the cycle of life in our suburban Chicago home, it was evident everywhere I looked in Yugoslavia, from my relatives' gardens and orchards to their chicken coops and farm animals. One of my earliest memories was the hot scream of a pig slaughtered during one of our visits, and it haunted me for years afterwards.

But it wasn't just the natural cycle of the seasons that got me—in Yugoslavia, I saw real, actual death, something I never experienced at home. When I was 10 years old, I nearly died from a severe case of salmonella I contracted from an ice cream shop on the Croatian coast. Because so many others had also been sickened, the hospital placed me into a contagious ward due to the overflow, where I was completely cut off from my family. I spent the next week dipping in and out of consciousness, watching the woman next to me die. At one point, I counted 56 puncture wounds in my arms from the blood tests and IVs.

When I was finally allowed out of bed, the other women in the ward took me under their wings. They were older, mothers with their own children waiting for them at home, and they taught me needlepoint to help pass the time, helped me with my rusty Serbo-Croatian.

Once I was well enough to walk, I could speak to visitors from our second-story window. In a scene straight out of a movie, objects were sent up and down in a wooden basket attached to a pulley. Below, visitors filled the basket with gifts of coffee and chocolate before sending it up to us.

As soon as I saw my mother standing below, I burst into tears. My new friends tried to comfort me, but it was my mother's arms I wanted around my shoulders, not theirs. At the age of 10, it was hard to not be able to touch her.

My mother came every day after that until they finally released me. And every day, she would send up gifts for my guardian angels, always a new bag of freshly ground coffee.

During that same trip to Yugoslavia, my cousin's wedding came to screeching halt when the best man was killed in a car accident. The traditional three-day, three-night-long wedding festivities immediately morphed into grief and mourning.

When I awoke the following morning, I heard wailing instead of the previous night's music and laughter. Women wore black, and men wore armbands. There would be no more music for six months, my mother told me. Heavy swaths of black cloth covered the mirrors, and preparations were already underway for the numerous upcoming church rituals.

In the days after my mother's death, I found myself yearning for such clear-cut rituals. I wished there was some way I could portray my grief without talking about it, that mourning black was still an accepted tradition, and that I had some kind of veil to separate me from the stark shock of the outer world.

More than anything, I wish we lived in a culture that respected grief. That didn't try to rush us past our feelings or encourage us to tamp them down. I was tired of having to say that my mother had just died, and I couldn't help but think how much easier it would have been if I had some outward sign of my grief. If someone saw me wearing black, they might recognize I was grieving, at which point they could either step up to support me, or stand back, to give me space.

Space and support were things I desperately needed—sometimes at the same time. And yet, I couldn't seem to ask for them. I was just too vulnerable, and I didn't know what I'd do if I finally worked up the courage to ask for support, only to be turned down.

When the priest said my mother's funeral service would be 10 or 15 minutes long, I didn't believe him. In my experience, it's pretty much impossible for a Serbian Orthodox priest to perform a short service. Sunday mass is at least an hour and a half long, and holiday masses usually last two to three hours. The first time I brought Ken to our church, it was for a midnight Easter mass, and he insisted we leave at 2:00 a.m., as the church was setting off fireworks. Not even the roasting pig being prepared for a dawn breakfast could incite him to stay.

So the priest's "Oh, it'll be short," comment should have been my first clue. The second was that we'd had no prior experience with the man. The priest my mother had favored had died a year or two back, and none of us, not even my mother, had forged a relationship with his replacement. And yet, this Orthodox church had been important to my mother—the closest she'd come to finding a church she called home since moving to Colorado from Chicago in the late 90s—so Marko and I had contacted them for the service.

The funeral went well enough for the first 20 or so minutes, until Father Gregory motioned for us to sit down. Then he really dug in, going on and on about how Milica had "fallen asleep," scaring the bejesus out of my four-year-old son, Gabriel. While Gabriel fought back tears, I started whispering in his ear, saying *Baba's not asleep, she's dead; don't pay any attention to what he's saying; it's not true, so don't let it scare you.*

But Father Gregory kept at it, singing *Oh Lord, Bless your handmaiden Milica, who has fallen asleep* as many times as he possibly could. Every single time, Gabriel would start crying again and I'd try to set him right, a one-woman anti-propaganda unit.

It was difficult enough to have lost my mother—no, to have been *burying* my mother—and I couldn't believe that the priest—the person who was supposed to be making this easier— was making the situation more difficult. The longer his intonations continued, the more upset I became. How desperately I wished we'd chosen another priest, even if he didn't represent the Serbian Orthodox faith.

Just when I thought things were finally starting to wind down, the priest started in on a new sermon, talking an additional 30 minutes about heaven, hell and the importance of denying oneself life's pleasures. By the time he started in on the graces of suffering, I was filled with an anger so hot that I felt like my head might explode.

I was sure I wasn't the only one feeling this way, and I looked around, trying to make eye contact. If I could find even one ally, I'd stand up and ask the priest to stop, tell him that we hadn't wanted such a sermon for my mother's service.

He wasn't *my* priest, so I wasn't worried about offending him. And now that my mother was dead, who was this service for if not for those of us left behind? If we'd wanted a traditional hell and brimstone sermon, we would have held the ceremony at the church, not beneath this great wide-open, forgiving sky.

But no one would meet my eyes. They were all looking down at the ground diminutively, like children who'd been scolded, and in that moment, I swore to myself I'd never again attend church. At least not *this* Orthodox church.

Nor would I raise my children under the banner of fear and judgment, tormented with the concepts of sin and hell. If simply for no other reason than I didn't believe it. Just like I didn't believe an unbaptized child would go to hell. When my mother had died, I'd looked death in the face, and God wasn't scary, like this priest was leading us to believe. God was beautiful, God was enormous and God was *loving*.

And God was forgiving.

This priest, I suddenly understood, didn't get it. He didn't understand that the real reason we were here was to love. We weren't here to live in fear, like so many of our religions taught. And we weren't here to judge ourselves or others. We weren't *meant* to live small lives in order to keep from burning in hell.

Later on, I found out that Marko had been so furious that he'd also vowed to never set foot in church again. Most of our friends were more democratic. It was a beautiful service, they told us, even if the priest had been a bit long-winded. Even if he'd scared the shit out of the children.

Thankfully, my mother's final request had saved the day. Years before, she'd asked us to play her favorite folk song, "*Ajde Jano*," while dancing around her casket. The song was about the joy of dancing and living in the moment, and it was the perfect antithesis to the priest's heavy-handed speech about suffering.

Ajde Jano, kolo da igramo.
Ajde Jano, ajde dušo, kolo da igramo.

Come on, Jana, let's dance the kolo.
Come on Jana, come on dearest, let's dance the kolo.

Come on, Jana, let's sell the horse.
Come on Jana, come on dearest, let's sell the horse.

Come on, Jana, let's sell the house.
Come on Jana, come on dearest, let's sell the house.

We'll sell them, just so we can dance.
We'll sell them, Jana dearest, just so we can dance!

The song contradicted everything the priest had just ser-monized, and I couldn't have been happier when I saw the look of shock on his face as we cranked the volume on the boom box. Milica—that poor little handmaiden—had struck again.

CHAPTER 2

OWLS AND OTHER MIRACLES

We buried my mother on Winter Solstice, the shortest day of the year. The day was gray and overcast, as it had been for my father's funeral 20 years before. That day had been bitter, empty and frigid. This one was mild, further tempered by the family and friends who surrounded me.

As we lowered my mother's casket into the earth, the sun broke through, shining radiantly upon us before sinking back into the clouds. Later, at the celebration of life we held at Marko's house, everyone buzzed about it, talking about the sun breaking through at that *exact* moment. That was *Baba*, they said, I could feel it.

Unlike the others, I hadn't felt my mother's presence. I'd been helping Gabriel throw dirt and flowers onto her casket when the sun broke free, and what I'd felt at that moment wasn't sorrow, but a deep calm. As everyone around us sobbed, Gabriel and I were calm, focused, present. What I most remember from that moment was a sense of completeness, awash in the knowledge that yes, we were burying my mother, but everything would be all right.

A few days later, our friend Barb, a professional photographer who'd taken photos of the service, sent over her photos. When we got to the photos from the casket, we gasped. There we are, Gabriel and I, throwing flowers onto my mother's casket, a halo of light around my head. A perfect halo of light around Gabriel's head.

We looked through those pictures again and again, trying to pinpoint the source of that light. At first, I tried to rationalize it as a glare, simple glint of afternoon sunlight. But if that had been the case, the angle would have been different. It might have bounced off our heads, or come in at another angle. Instead, it formed two complete circles—one around Gabriel's face, and one around mine.

What do you say when you're handed such a gift? Do you accept it, or do you rationalize it away? Do you say that yes, Barb's a professional photographer, but she must have messed up. Hell, her equipment must have messed up.

Or do you remember that in her 20-year professional career, she's had other instances where the divine has surged through her lens, taking momentary life? Do you come to the conclusion that maybe, just maybe, that halo was my mother's spirit, wrapping us in divine light.

As the funeral was winding down, our friends Mandy and Josh watched in astonishment as a large owl flew away from a tree behind us. No one else saw it.

After that, images of owls began to appear everywhere we looked. A close friend who'd flown in for the service brought owl sympathy cards with him. Owl cards began arriving in the mail. A friend sent us an early Serbian Christmas gift: it was an owl, of course. Then, when December was winding down, I opened up the new calendar I'd bought months prior only to discover an owl perched on January's page. Here it was now, in my kitchen, ready to haunt me wherever I went.

On it went. Small, seemingly insignificant images of owls appeared in all sorts of crazy places—gifts people sent, images I stumbled across. I couldn't help but wonder about the synchronicity. In literature, the owl is a traditional symbol of death, and to have been bombarded with so many owl images in such a short time felt like a confirmation from my mother, telling us she was all right.

My mother had always been a child of nature, so it wasn't a surprise to any of us that she'd send such an image. She'd even looked a bit like an owl with her big, inquisitive eyes and round reading glasses, as we often joked when she put those glasses on. There was only one thing that didn't make sense: hawks had always been my mother's favorite bird, not owls.

During the last few days of my mother's life, I prayed for her to find peace. I didn't pray for God to extend her life; she was already suffering too much for that. The last-ditch chemo attempt her doctors recommended had catapulted my mother into the active dying phase, and witnessing that level of suffering had been brutal. So I prayed for peace. That she might find peace within herself, peace within God or the afterlife, whatever that meant.

During those long, painful hospital visits, I'd taken to ducking into the hospital chapel when no one was around. Even though there wasn't an Orthodox cross among the various religious symbols on the walls, the chapel was a calm, neutral place that felt good to me. One afternoon, I found myself leafing through the notebook lying open on the nondenominational altar. After much debate, I added my own prayer: Dear God, I wrote, please help Milica find peace.

That was all.

A week later, we buried my mother in a cemetery adjacent to the Boulder Flatirons. The manager, Olga, showed us a handful of plots in various sections of the cemetery, but the one that most called to us was high on a hill, where a tree had recently been removed. Leslie and I immediately agreed it was the perfect plot for my mother.

The name of the section? The Garden of Peace.

A few days after that, I was rumbling around my office, wrecked by the knowledge that we had *two* sets of holidays to get through. With the Serbian holidays extending into late January, our family holidays were a marathon on the best of years. How we were going to make it through this year was anyone's guess.

Those were the thoughts threatening to suffocate my heart when something drew my attention to a little book on my bookcase. A jolt of electricity ran through me as I picked up Maya Angelou's *Amazing Peace: A Christmas Poem*, the book my mother had given me the previous Christmas. Here it was, waiting for me now, when I most needed it.

I flipped through the book, trying to ascertain its message. "Angels and Mortals," I read, "Believers and Nonbelievers, look heavenward and speak the word aloud. Peace."

After the tumultuous period following my father's death, I knew my mother's death would always be a defining moment in my life. This time around, I didn't want to burrow and pretend that the loss didn't matter, as I'd done with my father. Nor did I want to get trapped in guilt and regret, as I'd done when he'd died, further prolonging my grief and suffering.

This time around, I wanted to face my grief head-on. This time around, I wanted to grieve consciously. To do that, I decided I would give myself this entire first year.

A year's worth of time and space—that would be my gift to myself. One full year to dance with my grief, wrestle with it and welcome it.

When the dour-faced ICU doctor told me my mother had gone septic and might not survive that first night, my body snapped into fight-or-flight mode, and I started shaking from the adrenaline coursing through my system. During this state, your amygdala activates, flooding your body with adrenaline and cortisol and giving you a surge of energy to address the threat before you. In the old days, we used this energy to fight our attackers or flee from them. I wanted to do both.

As I've since learned, we can do all sorts of physically impossible things when we're in the thick of fight-or-flight. The one thing we *cannot* do is think clearly. Literally. The rush of chemicals cascading through our bodies makes it impossible.

And yet, many of us find ourselves in this exact mental state as we're being asked to make complex, life-changing decisions about our loved ones. At the same time, we're bombarded with highly complex medical terminology that we probably don't understand. Even if we do, we're likely to forget it. As one doctor told me, he expects his patients to only remember 10% of their conversation.

Ten percent.

As I was trying to make sense of what was happening, the ICU doctor continued talking, flooding me with arcane and ridiculously complex terminology. I remember staring at him, trying to figure out what kind of language he was speaking. Once I managed to pull myself together, I asked a slew of questions to clarify my mother's situation.

But what if I hadn't been so hell-bent on understanding him?

What if I'd been a first-generation immigrant with a tentative grasp of the English language? What if the only thing I'd understood was that my mother was about to die? Worse still, what if I'd missed his subtle clue telling me it was time to say goodbye?

These weren't idle questions. As the daughter of Yugoslav immigrants, these were the kinds of concerns that shaped my childhood. If the misunderstandings my parents faced on a daily basis weren't literal, they were often cultural.

There are so many levels to the way we communicate. There's what we say, what we mean, and then there's what we actually want. A non-native speaker might not understand such nuances, especially in a life-or-death situation. Neither might a person awash in adrenaline and sudden grief.

When Joan Didion's daughter was sick, she used information from two clinical journals (John F. Murray's *Intensive Care: A Doctor's Journal* and Stephen G. Waxman's *Clinical Neuroanatomy*) to communicate with her daughter's ICU doctors. But the terminology from Waxman's book was so confusing that it reminded her of a failed attempt to learn Indonesian.

Why, in this day and age, is it so difficult to understand our doctors? And why must we go to such extraordinary lengths in order to communicate with them?

When my father died 20 years ago, I simply accepted whatever the doctors told me. These days, that's no longer the case. And yet, it took me a *full week* to get a clear answer out of my mother's team of oncologists.

As my mother was actively dying, her primary oncologist—a woman who'd been out of town at a conference the previous week—sat down with us, looked us in the eye and told my mother that yes, another round of chemo might be able to prolong her life for another six months.

Meanwhile, the oncologist who'd been making regular rounds suggested that she might have another two months. Until then, he suggested that we move my mother into a nursing home so she could "recover" and "get stronger."

When I finally cornered him, he kept saying that my mother could live for another two months.

"You saw her in there," I said. "There's no way she's going to live another two months."

Silence.

I looked him in the eye, pleading. "My gut tell me she doesn't even have another two weeks."

He looked around before dropping his eyes. Finally, he sighed. "I think your instincts are right."

Why did this have to be so painful? Why did I have to waste my mother's final days arguing with a constantly-rotating set of doctors and their conflicting messages, second-guessing myself when I could have simply taken my mother home to spend her final days at home, as she'd wished?

These weren't new doctors, either. These were seasoned oncologists in their 50s and 60s who dealt with death on a daily basis. Surely, by now, they would have learned how to communicate clearly. Surely, by now, they would have learned the gift of compassion. Surely they would have learned the importance of choice, of allowing one to die as one wishes, with dignity.

Surely.

When it became clear that my mother wasn't going to bounce back from that last-ditch chemo attempt, Dr. Hudson—the doctor who'd saved my mother's life during that first, emergency surgery—nodded and told her to keep fighting. This was the doctor she'd seen most regularly in the following two months. The one doctor she looked up to, the only doctor she trusted.

And he looked her in the eye when he said it. Keep fighting.

So she did.

At some point, I'll be able to forgive these people. They're human, after all, and just as flawed and imperfect as the rest of us.

It's the current American medical model I can't forgive. The one that elevates its doctors to near-mythical proportions, pushing, prodding beyond any reasonable—much less humane—benefit. The one that snatches our precious last days with our loved ones as it insists they keep fighting, at all costs.

Never, ever give up, extols the current medical wisdom. As if death is a game, a battle that can be beaten. Something to be controlled, minced out and measured. Except this isn't how we live, not if we're being honest. And it shouldn't be how we die.

If there's a silver lining to this story, it resides in the clear and open communication we experienced with our hospice workers. From the instant my mother entered their jurisdiction, Marko and I felt like we'd finally received the honesty, clarity and direction we were seeking. Unfortunately, by the time we'd transferred my mother into their care, it was too late. Less than 24 hours after we moved her home, my mother was dead.

In 1997, my mother and I flew to Serbia to see my mother's closest sister, Andja, who was dying from cancer. The country was under heavy sanctions from its role in the Yugoslav wars, and basics such as aspirin weren't available. This didn't deter my aunt, who simply asked us to bring aspirin and vitamins from the U.S.

My aunt's health care was lacking as well. Her hospital was barely functioning, with deserted wards and burnt-out elevator lights, and it took hours for the nurses to respond to a single call. When they did, they were only able to provide minimal help, as I realized while stepping over a pool of blood from where a nurse had emptied a patient's tubing. The patients didn't seem to fare much better. The young woman in the bed next to my aunt had tossed and turned all night, *Teta* Andja told us, vomiting blood. By the time the sun rose, she was dead.

Despite this, my aunt was in good spirits, smiling her kind, mischievous, crinkly-eyed smile. "They're doing the best they can," she said of the nurses. "They don't have enough staff, and many of these nurses haven't even been paid."

Teta Andja shrugged. "That's life after war. It's not the leaders who struggle, but the people."

It was sobering to realize how different our lives in the U.S. were at the most fundamental level. In Serbia, a post-Socialist country whose infrastructure had crumbled, people were struggling, often without pay or enough food. Despite that, they had deep social networks, with extended families and neighbors working together to survive.

I'm not sure we have that luxury in the U.S. When Americans fall through the cracks, we tend to fall hard. When my parents' divorced and my father's business plunged into bankruptcy, I worked three jobs in high school just to keep food on the table. With Marko already off to college, there was no one to raise my mother and I from the ashes, and I knew it.

Despite this, my American life provided a better alternative than one of constant war. To my parents, who'd been brought up in World War II, the U.S. offered a sense of possibility that the former Yugoslavia never could. "You might not have enough to eat in the U.S.," my mother once observed, "but at least you'll never be bombed."

After a few days in the hospital, my aunt would spend a few days at home. She'd visit with the stream of neighbors who came to see her, then take a short walk around the garden before returning to bed. Here and there, she'd have some coffee with us, a bit of whiskey, maybe some soup. This was how she passed her final few weeks, going back and forth between her home and the hospital.

When my mother was dying, she spoke of this visit. "I didn't realize it at the time, but *Teta* Andja showed me something back there. Drink a little coffee, eat a little soup, walk around the garden. Go to the hospital for a bit, so they can take care of you, then come home, to visit with your loved ones."

I bent closer, tears in my eyes. *Teta* Andja had been my mother's favorite sister, and I knew how hard the loss had been on her.

"We'd be talking," my mother said, "and she'd say 'Give me a puff of your cigarette.'

"'Are you crazy?' I'd say. There she was, dying of cancer, and she still wanted a puff from my cigarette or a bit of whiskey. But she just laughed."

My mother nodded. "She taught me something that day. She taught me how to die with dignity."

The owl images continued to appear for much of the first month after my mother's death. As that first month was coming to a close, I found myself struggling emotionally. The intense waves of grief I'd felt since my mother's death no longer seemed to recede; they felt more stuck, stagnant.

In an attempt to move this energy, I buckled down on my self-care, writing and meditating as often as I could. And I brought my sorrow to my dance class, where I could kick and scream, laugh and cry—the one place I could totally *be*, no matter what.

My dance teacher, Juliet, had a gift for creating an atmosphere filled with joy and freedom, and even though I'd danced my entire life, I'd never attended a class like her Ayre class. The music was an uplifting mix of hip-hop, rap, R&B, disco and indie rock, and instead of criticizing or correcting us, as so many other teachers did, Juliet sang and laughed as she danced, freeing us to do the same.

Her class had helped bring me back from the brink of postpartum depression after Gabriel was born, and in the years since, I'd attended it religiously. Simply put, dancing helped me access emotions that I couldn't reach any other way. When my mother was dying, I went to class every day, crying when a particular song or movement hit another fragment of grief. Many days, I left early, in tears. That was OK. My bout with postpartum depression had taught me the importance of trusting my body and its wisdom.

On my way out of class one tumultuous morning after my mother's death, I reached into my purse to jot down some observation about my mother, and pulled out a journal. A writer friend had given it to me while my mother was sick, and in the chaos of the preceding months, I'd forgotten all about it.

In the safety of my car, I took a closer look. On the cover was a pensive-looking woman lying facedown on a couch. Long hair covered her face, and she appeared to be crying. It was me in a nutshell, and I stared at it for a moment, wondering about the synchronicity of finding this woman today, when I was drowning.

When I was done jotting down my thoughts, I flipped the journal over to the back. And what looked back at me, but another wise, omniscient owl.

My agitation continued. Dancing took the edge off momentarily, but there was something deeper going on, something I couldn't access. Meanwhile, Marko and I began discussing whether or not we were going to hold the traditional 40th day memorial service for my mother.

Despite my anger at the priest who'd presided over my mother's funeral, I didn't know if it was fair to my mother's spirit to cheat her out of this pivotal rite. Her faith had been important to her, and if I could find a way to honor that while staying true to myself, so much the better.

Even though I'd been raised in the Serbian Orthodox church, my main connection to the church had been through folk music and dance, not worship. As such, I'd had a much more casual relationship with the church than my mother. That only deepened after Nico, our first son, was born. My mom had wanted us to baptize him, but it didn't seem right to bring my son into a church where Ken wasn't a member. Besides, Ken and I were the spiritual but not religious types who valued the natural world over church doctrine.

Neither one of us thought it would be a big issue not to baptize Nico. But it was to my mom. So for months, I went back and forth about it. In the midst of this, we accompanied my mom to a church festival one bright Saturday morning in hopes of bridging the gap. Perhaps asking the parish priest some questions about the baptism might help allay my hesitation, I thought.

After perusing the booths and snacking on cheese *pita*, phyllo dough stuffed with cheese, I walked over to Father Douglas with nine-month-old Nico in my arms, full of optimism. It was a sunny spring morning and we'd been enjoying ourselves.

"Ah," Father Douglas said, eyes dilated into tiny points of light, "yes, yes, I know who you are. Your mother's heartbroken that you haven't baptized your son yet. I've been praying for him, that he doesn't go to hell."

I reeled back, a visceral sting spreading throughout my body. Here I was, inquiring about bringing my child into this man's church and *this* was his reaction?

As I stumbled away, I swore I'd never baptize my children into this man's church. Nor would I bring them into this place of judgment and fear. Furthermore, I fully believed that babies were born whole, perfect beings and for this priest to tell me my child was going to hell was wrong.

And just like that, I was done. Done with the church and a lifetime of fear, subjugation and judgment. The sinners-be-saved sermon Father Gregory subjected us to during my mother's funeral simply cemented those feelings. Holding the 40th day memorial service for my mother, I decided, would be my last exchange with this particular church. And my very last olive branch.

As we delved more deeply into the 40th day memorial service preparations, my research taught me that in Orthodox doctrine, the deceased's soul wanders for the first 40 days after his or her death, visiting people and places and saying goodbye. The 40th day service was when the spirit finally said goodbye, leaving this world forever.

That night, I broke down. I could handle my mother as a spirit; I could handle her visiting her favorite people and places one last time. Saying goodbye to her physical presence had been brutal enough, but an eternal goodbye to her spirit? Absolutely not. My heart wouldn't allow it.

On the Friday morning of my mother's 40th day service, Father Matthew, the new parish priest at my mother's church, was called out of town for an emergency. We would need to move my mother's memorial service to Sunday, he told us, following the regular mass.

Except that Sunday was *Sveti Sava*—the anniversary of Saint Sava, the founder of the Orthodox Church. It was one of the church's biggest holidays, and an event Marko and I had been trying to avoid.

There was no chance of that now, so we steeled ourselves as best as we could. When Sunday morning arrived, Marko and I piled our families into our respective cars, timing our arrival so that we'd miss the bulk of the regular Sunday mass. As we were trolling the streets of North Denver looking for a parking spot, I spotted Ken's friend Thomas toting his cello.

Thomas had played at our wedding as well as at the celebration of life we'd held after my mother's funeral, and it was hard to describe my happiness at seeing him. We'd planned to leave right after my mother's service, but now that Ken and I had spotted Thomas and the rest of his Balkan band, the post-mass *Sveti Sava* celebration suddenly didn't look so bad.

"Maybe we stay after all?" Ken said.

I nodded with excitement. Live Balkan music wasn't something you came across every day. "Let's see how it goes, though. If the kids start to freak out, I'm outta here."

We herded the children ahead and pressed inside the church. It was small, with only a handful of crowded pews, and like other Orthodox churches I'd visited, the church was a cacophony of light, color, sound and incense. Colorful icons covered the walls, patches of multicolored light streamed in from myriad stained-glass windows and atonal, dissonant hymns filled the air. While Ken bought candles, I showed Nico and

Gabriel how to cross themselves in the Serbian Orthodox fashion. Then we piled into the back of the church and waited for the mass to end.

Marko and I had gone to church regularly as children, and it felt good, somehow, or perhaps just familiar, to be back. I'd always loved the beauty of Orthodox churches, and when Ken and I had gotten married, I'd considered holding our ceremony here. But Ken was still traumatized from the two-hour-long Easter midnight mass I'd dragged him to when we were dating, and in the end, the Denver Botanical Gardens felt like a better fit for both of us.

After the Sunday mass parishioners filed out, Father Matthew beckoned us forward. He bent down and introduced himself to the children, joking about something or other, and I felt the armor around my heart melt, just a little. Father Gregory, the priest who'd performed my mother's funeral service, was also in attendance, as were two other priests I didn't recognize.

We gathered in front of the pews, close to the altar. Now that we were standing in the middle of the blood-red carpet, deep in a cloud of incense, I couldn't get over the intense sensory experience of this church, and I watched Nico and Gabriel as they looked around, wide-eyed. Their only other experience with church had taken place in the Buddhist temple where Ken's family had held his father's memorial service. That temple had been calm, muted, serene. By comparison, this church was much more animal and physical, almost surreal.

The actual 40th day memorial service for my mother was brief. I was ready for the hardcore sermon we'd heard at the funeral, but it never came. Father Matthew had a much lighter touch than Father Gregory, and I found the service surprisingly powerful and moving. Having *four* priests praying for my mother's soul in this cacophony of light, color and sound felt magical, and I knew my mother would have loved it.

As we were walking out of the church, I couldn't help but think how different my mother's funeral would have been with Father Matthew at the helm. Perhaps it wasn't the religion that had bothered me so much as the priest. Whereas Father Gregory had been patriarchal and absolute in his delivery, Father Matthew struck me as a kinder, gentler person, one who was comfortable in his own skin. The kind of person you could actually have a conversation with.

Marko agreed. All of us, in fact, were a bit shocked by how well the ceremony had gone, and we couldn't stop talking about it as we made our way over to the hall for the *Sveti Sava* festivities.

The party was another nice surprise, with the actual *Sveti Sava* program brief and to the point, decidedly unlike the programs from my youth. Afterwards, plates of cheese *pita*, one of my favorite childhood foods, were passed around the room, and the seven of us settled into one of the long rows of red-plastic-tablecloth-covered folding tables that filled the room.

While the kids dug into the *pita*, Marko bought us a round of beers from the bar. With full hearts, Marko, Leslie, Ken and I toasted my mother. We all agreed that she would have loved this celebration.

When the plates of *sarma* arrived, I had to take a minute to compose myself. *Sarma*, pickled cabbage leaves stuffed with meat and rice and cooked in a tomato-based sauce, was the only thing my mother had asked for in her final days, and it had nearly broken me that I hadn't been able to prepare it for her.

But making *sarma* depended on finding whole pickled cabbage leaves, something we hadn't been able to find in Denver. Here we were now, 40 days after her death, surrounded by an abundance of it. Another last request, filled.

As we dug into our meals, Ken and Leslie marveled over how well everything had turned out. Marko, meanwhile, motioned me over and introduced me to the woman sitting next to him—Danica, an old friend of my mother's. I looked at them in surprise; what were the chances that my mother's closest friend from church just happened to be sitting next to my brother?

After talking with Danica for a while, I went back to finish my meal. The kids were eating *pita* like there was no tomorrow, and as I relaxed into my seat, one of the priests sat down next to me. Father Seraphim was a big bear of a man with a giant head of curly white hair, and he and his wife intrigued me immediately. Father Gregory and his wife sat down across from them, and I sat up a little straighter, feeling guilty to be drinking a beer.

Father Seraphim's big, booming laugh soon put me at ease. He looked like a big, happy, gregarious Italian Santa, and he laughed every other second. In nearly every way, he appeared to be the antithesis of somber Father Gregory, and I couldn't help but like him immediately.

Father Seraphim (his real name) wasn't a typical Orthodox priest by any stretch. He'd been raised Catholic, was of Italian descent, and had been a Vietnam veteran as well as worked in information technology before becoming a priest. I was just about to ask him why he chose Orthodoxy when the music started in.

"*Ajde Jano*"—it was my mom's favorite song, the one we'd played as we danced around her casket. Marko and I locked eyes, both of us a with a *what-are-the-chances* look on our faces. When we'd hired this same group of musicians to play at my mom's wake, "*Ajde Jano*" was the only song we'd requested. But somehow, they'd played a Bulgarian version instead of the Serbian one, and it had been a source of lingering regret for both of us.

This time around, it was the right version.

This time around, it was the right *everything*.

I looked at Marko with glistening eyes. How much my mother would have loved this—all of it. The day had quickly become the giant send off she would've wanted, and I couldn't help but feel my mother's presence everywhere I looked. So many miracles. So much magic.

BOOK 2

RECKONING

My heart, sit only with those
who know and understand you.
Sit only under a tree
that is full of blossoms.

—RUMI

CHAPTER 3

ROOTS

Like most children of war, my mom didn't like to talk about her past. If pressed, she'd share a few stories about growing up during World War II, but the conditions had to be right. She had to be rested, in the right mood and there had to be coffee. These weren't conversations pressed into the edges of the day. My mother understood that.

Like other children raised by WWII survivors, my childhood was marked by a silence so dense that the past barely seemed to exist. As a sensitive child, I could sniff out my parents' pain in a heartbeat, even though I didn't understand it.

No one told me that my grandmother had been killed by bomb shrapnel when my father was just a young boy. And yet I could feel that deep wound within him. I saw it when he lashed out, criticizing my every move, and I saw it when he ran, unable to sit with any kind of conflict. Because I didn't have any other information, I deduced it was my fault. So I tried harder.

Always, I tried harder.

My mother had a different set of holes in her past. As often as I dared, I asked her to tell me how she and her family had been set free by Italian Partisans the night before they were to have been killed in a concentration camp by Croatian *Ustaše*. *They were planning to drown you all, right? Was it Red Lake or Blue Lake*, I'd ask. *And you were only two years old?*

During cheerier times, we'd ask for the crazier stories. *Tell us the story of how Ujko Jovo got a gold rib!* we'd shriek. *Tell me how Baba broke my uncle out of jail with a gun!*

Such stories swelled my pride and cemented my deeply rebellious future. The rest of my family legacy remained hazy, unclear. What had happened to my mother's father, my grandfather Nikola?

"Oh, him," she said, waving away my question. "He was shot by his cousin for his land."

"What?! He was shot by his *cousin?*"

"Well, that's how the story goes." My mother paused at my look. "Is it true? I don't really know."

I didn't get any more out of her until I had my own children. By then, I'd begun to press. What had happened between my mother and her father? Didn't she ever see him again after she moved to the U.S. at the age of 18? Didn't she miss him?

She'd written him a letter once, she said, after Marko was born. Telling him that he had a grandson. That had been her olive branch.

"What happened?" I asked breathlessly.

"Nothing. I never heard from him."

I let this wash over me.

"You never tried again? All those times we were in Yugoslavia, you never saw him? I never met him?"

She shook her head. "Although many years later, someone told me he showed them the pictures I sent of his grandson."

A deep ache spread throughout my stomach.

"That was it?"

My mother stood up. "He was a selfish man, Tanja. Enough of these stories. It's time to start dinner."

My father was an even more tightly guarded secret. When I was nine, I learned that he'd been married before my mother and that I had an older half-brother, Miki, who lived in Belgrade. This I learned as Miki was on his way to visit us for a month.

I didn't learn anything about my paternal grandmother until long after my father had left. My mother was the one who finally told me she'd died in WWII, and it took me years to track down the fragments of that story, as well as the sole remaining picture of her that still existed.

The story of my grandfather was even more tenuous. At some point after my father left, I learned that my grandfather had committed suicide. I knew this, somewhere in the back of my head, as children do, having picked up bits and pieces and subconsciously put them together over the years. But I'd thought my train conductor grandfather had shot himself in the head whereas he'd thrown himself onto the railroad tracks outside his house after learning his second wife had cheated on him. The symbolism was almost too much.

While my parents strove to forget, I fought to remember. Perhaps it'll come as no surprise that I became insistent on truth at all costs. After having spent my formative years chased by emotional demons none of us seemed to understand, shining a light on my family's stories became my sole path to freedom.

CHAPTER 4

RECKONING

When the owl images stopped, the hawks started. I was used to seeing the occasional hawk around town, but now I began to see them on a regular basis—on my drive to Gabriel's preschool, walking around the lake by our house, passing my mother's condo. They almost always appeared when I was having a bad day and missing my mother.

One afternoon, on my way home from a yucky meeting, I turned onto my street, wondering how I was going to pull it together enough to pick up the kids from school. As I neared my house, I spied a red-tailed hawk circling my driveway. Mouth hanging open, I craned to get a better view. There she was, my hawk, circling low, creating a perfect circle from my driveway to my neighbor's. One circle, two; then three, then four.

It wasn't long before hawk sightings became a kind of shorthand in my family, gifts that appeared on particularly bad days. We shared these sightings with due reverence—the hawk Marko saw on his hike, the hawk soaring above Leslie as she sped along the freeway, stressed out from work. The hawk, the hawk, the hawk.

A few weeks after my mother's death, Marko and I sat down to address the ever-mounting medical bills. The kids were back in school and we'd survived Christmas and New Year's. I remembered very little of any of it.

As the executor of my mother's estate, Marko was worried about the amount of money we owed. He'd turned my mother's dining room table into Command Central, and we hunkered down over the piles of bills, trying to make meaning where there appeared to be none.

I couldn't believe how much money my mother owed and my throat tightened with each new envelope. There were hospital bills, doctor bills, lab bills, rehab bills. We'd been advised that it would take months for the insurance to settle everything; in the meantime, we were already getting alarming letters from the hospital and rehabilitation center threatening to take us to court.

Thank God my mother had had Medicare. Without it, she would have drowned financially. My father had died broke, on Medicaid, and I wouldn't wish that on anyone.

Despite the Medicare insurance, the bills were beyond overwhelming. How was it possible that she still owed thousands and thousands of dollars? While Marko pulled out another bill, I picked up a letter from the University of Colorado Anschutz Medical Campus, where my mother had gone once to see a specialist named Dr. Christopher Lieu.

The letter was from someone in the financial division who'd reviewed my mother's records and thought she might be eligible for financial aid.

I held up the letter, a shining beacon of hope.

Marko shook his head. "I don't think that applies."

"Why not?" I asked.

"Well, she's already dead."

"But I can call and check."

"I don't know that it'll be of any use."

My heart sank. He was right, of course. A stroke of luck like this happened to other people; it didn't happen in my family.

We reviewed the stacks of bills for another hour before wrapping up for the day. I picked up the CU Anschutz letter on my way out.

"I don't know, Marko. I think this might actually help."

Marko looked up. "Go for it, if you want."

"Well," I shrugged, "the worst that can happen is that they say no."

Meanwhile, the 20th anniversary of my father's death was quickly approaching. Every year, it seemed to pummel me in some way, large or small, and this year was no exception. Coming so closely on the heels of my mother's death, this particular milestone was a reckoning. I'd come so far since my father's death— I'd become another person entirely—and yet I couldn't shake the thought that I was an orphan now that my mother had died, totally alone.

I had Ken, of course, and my children, but what I no longer had was a parent who'd be there for me, someone who'd take care of me no matter what. Someone who'd take care of me *right now.*

At the same time, I realized that I no longer had anyone's expectations to live up to. I no longer had to please anyone—I could finally be myself, rip off the layers I'd used to disguise myself over the years.

This hit me on a deep level, an intense personal reckoning. I was 42, feeling the early squeeze of midlife, if not an outright crisis. Whoever I was in the past was gone. The daughter I'd once been no longer existed. Who would step forth in her place? Would it be the real me, or another imposter?

American psychologists often encourage us to maintain clear boundaries with our parents, particularly if the relationship is troubled. The therapist I turned to during a traumatic breakup in graduate school lauded my decision to live in a different town than my mother. Keep your boundaries, he said. Make your visit shorter, and if need be, minimize your visits home.

But what this doesn't do is *heal* the relationship. It only teaches us how to manage it, often painfully at best. And it gives us the illusion of control.

What I've found is that all of that is bullshit. Because even if we only see our parents two or three days of the year, all of those same family dynamics are still there, waiting for us. If they weren't, why would our parents trigger us so easily?

Like most mothers-daughter relationships, my relationship with my mother was fraught with tension. After she died, I wondered if some of that tension stemmed from the belief that we weren't good enough and never could be, not in our patriarchal and misogynist ethnicity. My mother's challenges went far deeper than mine, though; at the age of 12, she was "promised" to an aunt in America who didn't have children.

I can't imagine what it would be like to spend your teenage years waiting to move to another country so that you can become the makeshift child (and worker bee) someone never had. The youngest girl of eight children, my mother's only concept of America before she moved to Chicago stemmed from movies; like many 18-year-olds, she believed her new life would be marked by freedom and love, maybe even a handsome, young prince.

The prince she found was my father, a man so hell-bent on escape he'd already deserted one wife and child in Yugoslavia before moving to Paris to become a photographer. By the time they met on the South Side of Chicago, he was running his own photography studio—something I imagine my literature-and-music-loving mother found appealing.

Is that what drew them to each other? From brief conversations over the years, I don't think it was love. Perhaps a shared heritage and language were more important in those days. After all, he was Serbian, too; one of her people. I'm guessing she thought she could trust him.

It would take her years to learn that you can't trust someone who doesn't trust himself.

After I left home for college in 1988, I spent 14 years moving around the country, running from my family of origin, with few changes in our mother-daughter relationship to show for it. Even though my mother and I loved each other deeply, we were both headstrong and independent, and despite frequent visits, our path to harmony remained short-lived.

I'd always craved a deeper connection with my mother, and part of the way I fulfilled that was by exploring my heritage in my 20s. Both of my parents had such harrowing childhood war stories that I could barely bend my mind around them. And yet, even then, I knew that unearthing the past was my key to freedom.

So I kept digging. I supplemented my undergraduate English degree at the University of Wisconsin-Madison with Serbian/Bosnian/Croatian language and literature classes, and I did the same at Indiana University, where I earned my M.F.A. in Creative Writing. I did this to better understand my parents and their histories, but also to better understand myself. And I kept writing as Yugoslavia blew apart around me, delving into the shock of watching my relatives' cities being bombed on the news, horrified by the knowledge that my ethnic group was committing some of the worst atrocities of the 20th century.

This was my path during the 90s, and it culminated with me spending the 2001-2002 academic year in Slovenia writing a novel on a grant. The novel was about an American woman of mixed Yugoslav heritage caught in the former Yugoslavia during NATO's 1999 bombing of Serbia, and I worked on it furiously during my final year of grad school as well as during the nine months I spent in Slovenia.

Then I moved to Belgrade in hopes of finding a job with a non-governmental organization and staying abroad for another year. For most of my life, I'd felt torn between my American and my Serbian selves, and spending a year in Belgrade, I'd decided, would be my showdown. Now that my novel and my graduate school degree were complete, I wanted to see if I could do the reverse migration my parents had done, effectively reclaiming my heritage and some lost, unknowable part of myself in the process.

After having spent my childhood helping my parents navigate the subtle and often-complex customs and beliefs of their adopted country, I assumed I was prepared to move to a country I already knew. I couldn't have been more wrong. As an unmarried, independent woman with strong American beliefs, I stuck out like a sore thumb, and despite my best efforts, I wasn't able to find a job or a social circle. I left Serbia three months later with the clear knowledge that I no longer belonged in the former Yugoslavia, defeated at my core.

I was 32 years old when I returned to the United States, and deeply unmoored. I flew into Boulder, where Marko, Leslie and my recently-transplanted mother lived, planning to spend the next few months with them as I applied for academic positions around the country.

And then life stepped in. Marko and Leslie's daughter Maya was born a few weeks after I arrived, and shortly thereafter, my mother discovered that she needed heart surgery. With no family of my own and no job to tie me down, I became her caregiver.

After dropping Gabriel off at preschool one morning, I finally worked up the courage to call about the CU Anschutz financial aid letter. My heart was in my throat as I tried to explain why I was calling.

"But my mother's dead now," I said, "so I don't know if the letter still applies. I don't know if we're still eligible for your program."

"Oh no," Manuel, the kind man on the other side of the line, said, "it certainly applies. I'm glad you got in touch."

The Colorado Indigent Care Program (CICP) classification was retroactive, he explained. Once we filled out the appropriate paperwork and my mother was approved, she would become eligible for reduced fees at the CU Anschutz Medical Campus.

"In addition, she'll also be eligible for reduced fees at participating hospitals in the state of Colorado." Pause. "Assuming she was admitted to other hospitals during her illness."

"*Was she.*"

The rest of our conversation was a blur of thank-God-type-adrenaline as I frantically jotted notes. According to Manuel, the paperwork would identify my mother as indigent, and the CICP classification would help forgive the bulk of her hospital bills. Once we received the official classification, there were a few additional steps we had to take to apply the classification to Boulder Community Hospital. But that shouldn't be a problem, he said, as they were members of the program, too. We'd still be responsible for the remainder of the bills, but this would help quite a bit.

He would email me the CICP forms this afternoon. Did I have any questions?

My head was spinning. "You really think she'll qualify?"

"According to my paperwork, she will." He asked a few more questions to determine that my mother didn't have additional income beyond Social Security, such as stocks or bonds.

"Any inheritances," he asked, "or anything like that?"

I nearly laughed. If he only knew what my mother had been through these past few decades. Her retirement income was so low that for years I supplemented it with a monthly check just so she could make ends meet.

After we hung up, I paced around the kitchen, trying to wrap my head around this new turn of events. If what Manuel said was true, this wonderful man had just saved us thousands and thousands of dollars in hospital bills. My head was on fire.

I picked up the phone and called Marko.

He didn't believe it at first, either. He asked a slew of questions, trying to find a loophole. As far as I could tell, there weren't any.

"Look," I said. "This is a gift—don't you see? A giant, giant gift." My throat started to close up. "Somebody up there's watching out for us."

Money had always been an issue in my family. It was the final straw that led to my parents' divorce, and a life-long noose around both of my parents' necks. For immigrants such as my parents—people without extended family ties and support systems—money could be the difference between life and death.

It didn't help that my father had bankrupted his tool and die manufacturing business during the 80s, or that my parents had fought tooth and nail over what little remained during their nasty, four-year-long divorce. Once the divorce went through, things just got worse. By the time I was 17, I was working three jobs to help my travel-agent mother keep food on the table.

Meanwhile, my father had long since faded into a bitter stranger I no longer knew. Our twice-yearly meetings were characterized by stories so depressing that no one but me seemed to believe them. By the time I'd become a first-generation college student at the University of Wisconsin-Madison, my father was sleeping on a sheet of cardboard at his shop. Instead of sharing this with my new college friends—people whose parents regularly visited them, not to mention sent money—I withdrew even further into myself. Filled with a palpable shame, I spent my days juggling bar and restaurant jobs with my work-study office job, arguing with the bursar over why I needed more financial aid.

Once Manuel sent me the CICP paperwork, I submitted it as quickly as I could. Even though he'd reassured me that we'd be approved, I remained worried. There was just so much at stake.

True to his word, the approval came through quickly. Like me, Marko remained wary. Even though CU Anschutz had accepted my mother's CICP status, he wasn't sure that Boulder Community Hospital would.

"Can you just walk the paperwork over there and talk to someone?" I asked.

"Yeah," Marko said, "but what if they don't take it?"

"This is starting to remind me of that whole affordable housing thing last year," I said. "Remember?"

We'd spent the year before my mother's death getting her into Boulder's Affordable Housing program. It was the only way we could get my mother a nice but affordable condo in Boulder's highly-priced market—a move of increased importance since she'd fallen and broken her hip the previous year. Moving her into a first-floor condo had looked nearly impossible until we found the program.

Except we'd dragged our feet at the end of the process, and as we were getting ready to submit the final round of paperwork, we found that a pivotal rule had changed for the following calendar year. It was late December of 2011, just days before the New Year kicked in, and suddenly we didn't know if the small cash gift we'd given my mother so that she could afford the condo now negated her eligibility.

We went into crisis mode. My mother all but shut down, saying she knew it was too good to be true. She shouldn't have believed that she'd finally get such a nice place. With Ken's encouragement, I insisted we follow through. We'd spent the past year submitting paperwork and jumping through hoops to get my mother this condo, and damned if we were giving up in the final hour.

The CICP bill forgiveness very much felt like a similar fight.

"C'mon," I urged Marko. "We can *do* this. We got the condo for Ma, remember? We can get this money, too. Really."

As February descended, my grief deepened. Why was I making such a big deal of my father's anniversary now, 20 years after he'd died? I didn't yet understand that grief brings up old grief, and before long, I gave in to the feelings and let myself retreat from the world as much as I could. Meanwhile, I tried to figure out how the hell I could possibly commemorate my father's anniversary in a meaningful way.

My father had died the day before Valentine's Day, and ever since, I'd made a big show of ignoring the holiday. But this year, I'd been tasked with helping Nico make valentines for his first-grade homework project, and I couldn't ignore how excited the kids were about the holiday.

"Mama," Nico said to me that night over dinner, "why don't you and Daddy ever give us valentines?"

Ken and I looked at each other.

I mumbled something about my father dying and how that made me sad and even I realized how lame it sounded as I was trying to talk my way through it. It had been 20 years already. Why was I still carrying this anti-Valentine's-Day torch?

"You're right, Nico." I cleared my throat. "From now on, let's celebrate Valentine's Day. What should we do?"

The kids wanted to go to Sushi Zanmai, our special occasion restaurant. I looked at Ken.

"Well, it's not like we celebrate Valentine's Day very often," he said. "Let's do it!"

While Ken occupied the kids, I sprinted upstairs and quickly made Nico and Gabriel a hand-made valentine.

Nico, satisfied, tossed his aside to go play something else, and I stood there for a moment, thinking how easy it is to make a kid happy. We adults, now that's another story.

My sadness over the loss of my father usually started to ease after the anniversary of his death had passed, but this year it hung on. I couldn't get over the feeling of having become an orphan, and it colored everything I did and saw. I felt deeply, intensely alone.

By the end of February, I was starting to worry. Why wasn't this feeling gone? What did it mean?

One morning, Ken came down from his shower to find a small falcon standing outside our front door, waiting. For a few minutes, they looked at each other. Was the falcon hurt, he wondered? Did it need help?

By the time he called me over to see, the falcon was gone.

As I was struggling to understand my feelings, my friend's mother died. When Kathleen got back into town from the funeral, I was startled by how happy she looked. I was ready with condolences and *what-can-I-dos*, but Kathleen shook me off. She didn't need them.

"Watching her die was the most beautiful thing," she said, smiling. "Well, you know."

I smiled wanly. Somewhere along the way, I'd lost this simple truth. Not only that, but I'd become broken since my mother had died, increasingly vulnerable and afraid of death, and I deeply envied my friend. She was glowing, the essence of love and peace.

Had I looked like that after my mother had died? No wonder friends had given me startled looks when they'd come to the celebration of life that Marko and I had thrown after the burial, and they'd found us smiling and dancing.

In just over a month, I'd lost that magic—that deep, ingrained knowledge that everything was beautiful, just as it should be. I'd lost my connection to the divine.

My mood went from bad to worse. I wasn't taking ample time or space for myself, and it was showing. I was waking up in a funk, snapping at the kids and feeling pressed upon in every way imaginable. Getting the kids to school had become a drama unto itself, with me snapping and Nico crying on what seemed to have become a near-daily basis.

Things with Gabriel weren't much better. He'd reverted back to the clinginess he'd shown as my mother was dying, and getting him to preschool had become its own production, with him afraid to leave my side, and me afraid I'd blow my top.

Things had to change—even I could see that. Over the years, I'd learned that I needed to write, meditate and exercise in order to stay grounded. When I didn't, things got ugly, fast. During times of crises, these non-negotiables became even more important. Clearly, it was time to pull out the big guns.

I was already writing like a madwoman, jotting notes about my mother's illness and death on every surface I came across, but now I started getting up earlier in order to have some dedicated writing time each morning. Except that Nico had begun to wake earlier as well, meaning there was no transition time for me to pull myself out of grieving-daughter mindset and back into functional-mother mindset. It didn't seem to matter how early I got up—he was always there.

I didn't understand what was going on until my therapist Arielle explained that children need us most when we're emotionally unavailable. Give him some one-on-one time in the morning, she counseled, and he'll settle down.

So we struck the following bargain: Nico and I would have 30 minutes together every morning, from 6:00-6:30 a.m., before Gabriel woke up. And I would get up at 5:30 a.m. to meditate and get grounded before starting my day. If Nico woke up earlier, he could read in his room or do whatever he wanted. This helped us both immensely. I got to have time for myself and Nico got to have one-on-one time with me before school.

Meanwhile, I stared spending the 5:30-6:00 a.m. slot doing the online meditations I'd found on *Yogaglo*. I often chose David Wagner's meditations for loss or sadness, and would sob my way through them as I struggled to get a foothold on my grief.

At first, I wasn't sure if this was helping or hindering my mental health. Was diving this deeply into my grief just making it worse? I knew plenty of people who believed it was better to simply move on.

But that wasn't how I lived, not any more. After having spent the first 29 years of my life stuffing my feelings and running from everyone and everything in my life, the shit finally hit the fan during a nasty graduate school break up. All of my family issues rose to the forefront, particularly my unresolved issues with my father. I ended up in therapy for the first time in my life, where a kind therapist named Andrew helped save my life.

That god-awful experience taught me that old, unresolved pain always comes out, no matter how long it takes. The harder we try to stuff those unbearable feelings down, the worse it looks when things finally explode. Which is why I'd become such a big believer in feeling my emotions over the years. The more I could let my emotions rise to the surface, the easier it was for me to release them.

But my grief over my mother's death wasn't following any of those patterns. It seemed interminable. It caught me coming and going. The best I could do was to work my way through my grief each morning, knowing it would catch me again that afternoon. Meanwhile, the momentary peace I felt after stumbling through one of Wagner's meditations felt like a giant gift. For a few minutes, I could breathe again. For a few minutes, I felt like myself, even.

In this way, I was able to get grounded enough to get myself through the first part of the day and get the kids off to school. A few times a week, I danced off another layer of sadness in my dance class.

I was vigilant about this level of self-care because I had to be. With a grandfather who'd committed suicide and a scary episode of postpartum depression after Gabriel was born, I'd learned that writing, meditating and exercising were critical to my emotional health. My work with Arielle had taught me that. I'd found her after Gabriel's high-risk pregnancy and premature birth had pushed me into a full year of sleeplessness and I'd nearly caved from the stress.

And yet, many days I just didn't feel like going to my dance class. My grief was simply too exhausting. But like the meditation videos I'd been doing, I knew myself well enough to know that this was something I couldn't drop. So I pulled on my dance clothes anyway.

On low-functioning days, I simply left class early. Some days, I looked at the clock as the first song started, telling myself: 20 minutes. I can stick with this for 20 minutes. Sometimes, I left halfway through. More often than not, I left in tears.

I remember an acquaintance telling me that she cried every day of that first year after her father died and I wasn't much different. Waves of grief would hit me at the strangest times, and I often broke into tears at the slightest hint of my mother's illness or death. Driving past my mother's hospital after I'd dropped Gabriel off at preschool clobbered me, as did certain songs in my dance class. For months, my car served as my go-to shelter, a safe place for me to cry when I was out and about.

Late afternoons often found me in bed, taking a few minutes away from the kids as that late-afternoon winter sun started to sink down across the horizon, my heart breaking afresh. During that late-afternoon crash, crawling into bed was one of the only things that helped. The other was my dog, Loki, who'd push open the door and settle in below my feet. Loki had always followed me around, and after my mother's death, he seemed to keep an especially close eye on me.

For months, I lived in old, ratty dance clothes topped by a soft, blue fleece jacket. In another year, I'd barely be able to look at that jacket, but for now, I hardly took it off. I craved comfort on every level.

My father was a critical man, chased by his own demons, and it took me years to understand how deeply that double-edged sword of criticism must have cut toward himself. I was 22 years old when he died from colon cancer, and his death broke me on multiple levels. Heartbroken that I'd never been able to repair my relationship with him, I punished myself for not having done enough, not having been good enough. Surely, I should have found some way to have earned his love. It would take me years to understand that earning a parent's love isn't a job in most families, but a birthright.

His death became a catalyst in my professional life as well. Determined to learn from the mistakes he'd made bankrupting himself, his company and our family while chasing material success, I quit the white-collar publishing sales job I'd taken out of college and went back to tending bar until I could figure out what I wanted to do with my life.

Never again would I take a job solely for the money, I decided. Instead of chasing the material success that had imprisoned my father, I would live a life of meaning. The last thing I wanted to do was follow in my father's footsteps, dying an early death, with nothing but a handful of broken dreams to show for it.

Between the CICP paperwork and the medical bills, Marko and I were speaking multiple times each day. Because Marko's job allowed him to work from home, he was able to knock out bits and pieces of the estate chores during odd moments. In addition to settling my mother's outstanding bills, Marko wanted to sell the condo immediately. As the executor of my mother's estate, he wanted this task finished while I couldn't even think about selling it. The condo had become a place where I could go to connect with my mom, and I wasn't willing to give it up. Couldn't we wait a few months, I asked, at least until we get all of the bills cleared up?

Our conversations swirled around logistics and to-dos when all I wanted was to focus on my grief, not figure things out. After a few weeks of this, I had to start putting some boundaries around our conversations, such as not answering the phone when I was with the kids—it was just too upsetting to talk about my mother's medical bills when I was back in mom mode. To survive, I needed to compartmentalize parts of my life.

Regular, daily life continued to move quickly, without enough space, without enough time. Some days felt like I was living the movie *Groundhog Day* over and over: wake up, feed the kids, get Nico to school, get Gabriel to preschool, write briefly, hit my dance class, pick up Gabriel, prepare lunch, play with him, pick up Nico, homework, dinner, dishes, bed. Since Gabriel was only in preschool for three hours a day, three days a week, I often felt crunched for space and time, and this made me resent Marko's calls even more.

I found myself choking under the weight of responsibility, jealous of the space and solitude Marko had working from home alone. At the same time, I knew that sitting in an empty home by myself all day would have destroyed me.

And so I continued to chafe against the very real demands on my time and attention, wishing, always wishing, that someone or something would save me.

The more estate tasks that were on my to-do list, the higher my level of anxiety and the more often I went to my dance class. When my mother was dying, the only way I'd been able to control my sky-high anxiety was by going every day. Like some of the other moms, I'd taken to bringing my kids to class with me when I didn't have childcare. They sat out in the hallway and played while we danced. We formed a not-so-secret union: moms who knew our emotional and physical health depended on getting our asses to class.

That dynamic continued to ring true for me, and whenever I looked like I was about to snap, Ken would ask if I'd been to my dance class recently. The days I wasn't able to exercise tended to be dark. When my exercise regimen slid, the rest of my self-care did, too, and it only took a day or two of this before I started to shut down. Then, when I snapped at Ken or the kids because I hadn't taken care of myself, I felt ashamed, convinced I was the worst person on the planet.

Much later, I read an essay by Sobonfu Some on the importance of feeling our grief. When we don't allow ourselves to feel our grief, she wrote, we often lash out at others. Check, and check.

After lashing out at my loved ones, I'd crawl away in shame. All I needed to do was try harder, damn it. Trying harder had saved me before. It would save me again.

It took me almost 10 years to heal the wounds of my father's death, and I spent the first four of those tending bar. Years that were a sort of treading water, gathering strength. I had always had a deep love of writing and reading, and after my father's death, writing about my family began to give my life structure and meaning. I wrote before I went to work at the bar, and I wrote after I came home. The words poured out of me, raw and broken, as I wrote about the past.

I wrote about who my father was, where he'd come from and everything that had happened between us. I wrote to fill the spaces, and I wrote to understand the gaps. I was determined, once and for all, to unearth the old family secrets—my parents had spent their lives running from them, and damned if I was doing to let them destroy my life as well.

Slowly, ever so slowly, I began to realize why it had been so hard for my father to open his heart; why he'd spent his entire life running, chasing one dream to the next. He'd been a young child when his mother had been killed by bomb shrapnel in southern Serbia in WWII, and I don't believe he ever fully recovered. His father remarried shortly afterwards, and he lived with a wicked stepmother who, as the story goes, despised him and his brother. By the time my father was 18, he was married with a child. From there, it was one escape to the next: Paris,

New York, then Chicago. My mom, our family, then the divorce; the third wife, then death.

My dance teacher was joyful and carefree in a way I ached to be. Juliet was the most nonjudgmental dance teacher I'd ever followed, and I wished I could be more like her. After having struggled with self-judgment and criticism my entire life, I was ready to toss those traits out the window. I just didn't know how.

Except for when I danced. Then I could sink into the magic of class, let the music carry me while I laughed and danced, kicked and yelled. The class was a gift: 60 minutes to get back to myself—the real me, who'd been buried for years. Finally, a place where I could be free.

After my mom died, my class became serious mind-body therapy. Once, after seeing how distraught I was to have been caught crying in class, a friend reassured me.

"We all cry in here at some point," she said. "Dancing brings it out. Look around when we're cooling down and you'll realize you're not the only one with tears in your eyes."

At a time when no one and nothing else could, my dance class held me.

When I allowed myself to process my grief by letting my sadness rise up and move through me, I felt better. At certain moments, life even felt manageable. Arielle had taught me another trick for reconnecting with my kids and I did my best with that, spending 15 minutes with my kids at least once or twice a week, playing whatever they wanted. The trick was to let them lead, and not try to control anything. For Gabriel, this meant chasing him around the house, slam-dunking our way through numerous basketball hoops. My time with Nico, meanwhile, was spent playing complex LEGO games of his choice. All I had to do was be fully present—no checking email or trying to multi-task. At first I didn't believe that twice a week would be enough, but I was astonished to learn how magically this repaired our relationships.

Now that the kids and I were having some good one-on-one time, I wasn't feeling quite so shitty about destroying their young psyches. This made it easier for me to continue getting up early to meditate and generally shoring up my self-care.

Things weren't going quite so well with Ken and I. We were fighting a lot, and I was getting all pissy about all sorts of things that probably wouldn't have bothered most people. In some ways, he was too easy of a target simply because he wasn't a child who needed my attention. He was an adult, and thus fully capable of taking care of himself.

That was what I told myself, anyway. Except that Ken wasn't doing particularly well, either. He had ulcerative colitis, a nasty autoimmune disease characterized by internal bleeding, and he'd flared up the same weekend my mother nearly died during that early emergency surgery. Ever since, he'd been getting steadily worse.

Ulcerative colitis is an incurable disease not easily managed. Over the years, I'd watched Ken's GI doctors catapult him from medicine to medicine, none of which seemed to help. Despite that, Ken managed to get his colitis into remission at some point or another. Some years, this took weeks; other times; months. When Ken's father was dying of lung cancer, Ken's colitis spiraled out of control for over a year.

Not surprisingly, Ken's colitis often flared up as the rest of us were tanking. It happened in 2010 when Gabriel was diagnosed with a life-threatening food allergy and it happened again in 2011 when my mother fell and broke her hip as Ken's father was dying.

Since Ken and I both worked from home, we were around each other more than most couples, which only magnified our dynamic. Instead of being flexible in our giving and receiving, one of us slunk off emotionally for a few days, weeks or months while the other spouse kept things together. Somewhere in there, we'd switch roles. Meanwhile, whoever was manning the home front was getting more and more resentful, until he or she finally blew up.

What a mess we were in. Even worse than our current emotional upheaval was the knowledge that Ken's ulcerative colitis, if left unchecked, could eventually lead to death.

This frightened me deeply, and I was livid that Ken wasn't taking better care of his emotional and physical health. I couldn't see that he was tanking just as I'd tanked, without the wherewithal to step back and assess how to get back on track. And I was so incensed about the whole situation that I couldn't give him what he most needed: empathy and compassion.

To complicate matters, I saw a clear connection between Ken, who stuffed his feelings, and my father, who'd done the same. Since my father had died of colon cancer and my husband was battling a disease of the colon, it was all too easy to think my husband was headed down the same path.

And then there was my mother, who'd died of appendiceal cancer, another disease of the colon. Three of the most important people in my life, all sickened by life-threatening diseases of the colon. What were the chances? I didn't see it as a coincidence, and found it highly suspect that all three had had a hard time expressing their emotions. That all three had effectively shut down their emotional selves, then suffered because of it. Damned if I was going to lose Ken as well simply because he refused to deal with his emotions.

And yet, that didn't come easily for him. I guessed it had something to do with Ken's Japanese American heritage, which valued group harmony over individual need, but it could just as easily have been the pressure of being male in America, where boys are taught to suck it up and "act like a man" at all costs. So round and round we went in our hellish little dance—me pushing Ken to feel his feelings, and him retreating further and further away.

This was the default pattern we'd fallen into in our relationship, one we both knew didn't work. Even though we'd gotten better at managing it over the years, we hadn't quite managed to break it. And if I'd learned anything these past few years, it was that Ken's health was *his* responsibility, not mine. No matter how hard I tried to save him, getting healthy was Ken's responsibility, not mine.

I knew all this. God, I knew it, but that didn't mean I understood it. So I fought my feelings toward Ken's colitis on a daily basis, wondering why the fuck Ken was sick again *now*, when my mother was dead and I needed him more than anything. A new level of resentment layered itself atop the old, pushing me further and further away from my husband.

One especially pissed-off day, I walked into my dance class trailing a giant cloud of anger. I could feel the stink of it following me around, covering me in shame as I settled into my spot. I didn't even make eye contact with anyone in case I inadvertently passed it on. The opening strains of Michael Kiwanuka's melancholy song "Home Again" floated through the loudspeakers. My stomach tightened.

Fuck.

Not The Death Routine. Not today.

For a minute, I almost ran out of class. I hated this routine, absolutely hated it. Of the dozens of routines Juliet taught, I hated this one because it included so many songs about loss. She'd started teaching the routine as my mother was dying, and every fricking time I heard those songs, I found myself right back in the hospital with my dying mother. When Wyclef Jean sang "I wish death never had a name," I often had to run to the bathroom before I broke into sobs.

Not-so-ironically, The Death Routine often showed up when I was doing my damnedest not to feel my grief. When I'd convinced myself I was fine, *fine damn it*, and was rushing through the logistics of my busy day.

Like today. So I took a deep breath, moved to the back of the room, where I could escape if I needed to, and begged my body not to turn on me. Please help me release whatever needed to be released, I prayed. And please help me make it through this class. Please.

By the time I left class, I'd escaped to the bathroom twice. But that was OK. I could feel something moving around in my chest again. I could breathe.

I climbed into my trusty bat-mobile and made my way home, glad to have survived another day.

Since illness seemed to be the predominant theme in our lives during this period, we were also making regular visits to the pediatrician. The stress from the last few months had sidelined us all, and after a nasty round of croup, both Gabriel and Nico got hit with strep throat. In the first six weeks after my mother's death, I was at the pediatrician's office *five* times.

This was beyond brutal because the pediatrician's office was in the same medical complex as the hospital, only 100 feet down the hall from the cancer ward where my mother had spent her final days. Every time we went to the pediatrician, I found myself bombarded with memories and images from the last week of my mother's life.

The cancer ward stood perpendicular to the wing that housed our pediatrician, and every time I passed it, I found myself unable to withdraw my gaze from the cancer ward windows. Each window housed its own sick and weakened soul, and one terrible afternoon, I saw my mother's gaunt and sunken face staring back at me. For an endless, heart-wrenching moment, I stared at my mother's ghostly face while Gabriel pulled my arm, convinced I'd lost my mind and was looking straight into a window from the past.

A few minutes later, I broke down to the pediatric nurse, blubbering about how hard it was to come here so soon after my mother's death. Why did their office have to be on the *same floor* as the cancer ward? Why couldn't it at least be in another section of the complex instead of just being down the hall?

And how come I had to bring my children in—not once or twice, like normal people—but *five fucking times* since my mother had died.

Janet listened kindly, nodding at all the right moments. One of the other nurses had gone through a similar process after her husband died, she said. He'd also had cancer, and had died just down the hall.

And then she had to come in to work after he passed. "Imagine having to *work* here," she said, "and having to come here every day."

I grunted.

"Don't worry," she said, "it'll get easier."

Gabriel's strep test came back positive, and after Janet sent in his antibiotic prescription, the doctor sent us home. On the way to the car, Gabriel started singing a song that he'd discovered shortly before my mother's death.

Step on a crack, break your mother's back.

I held his hand tightly every time he jumped, doing everything I could to keep from landing on a goddamn crack.

CHAPTER 5

THIS OPEN HEART

A few months after I arrived in Boulder in the fall of 2002, my mother underwent open-heart surgery to repair a leaking mitral valve. When I went to see her in the ICU shortly after her surgery, she looked dead. Her face was grotesquely bloated and misshapen from the fluids they'd pumped into her during surgery, and the sight shocked me to my core. It was one of those pivotal moments that turn your life around, and right then, I vowed I would do whatever I could to save her.

I was 32 years old, fresh from graduate school and my year abroad, and suddenly, none of that mattered. I was done running, and I knew it. So for six weeks after she came home, I cooked and cleaned for my mother, as well as took her on twice-daily laps around the parking lot. I helped her up and down her steep condo stairs, carrying anything heavier than five pounds to keep her chest sutures from coming apart.

Those months were equal parts hell and healing. For someone who'd always lived with an escape hatch, my new life contained minimal freedoms. After 14 years of living independently, I was now driving my mother's car and sleeping on her couch. At the same time, I was seeing my mother getting stronger with each new day. With that strength came the not-so-subtle return of our old patterns—that age-old need for independence, both of us lashing out at each other in frustration and judgment.

In my free time, I pursued academic jobs for the following year, sending out cover letters and packets of supporting material to universities around the country. Thus I endured this limbic time, trapped in a surreal version of my childhood, waiting for some phantom English department to decide my fate. I would take whatever academic position was offered, move to whatever city housed this new life. That was what academics did, after all; it was what I'd trained for. In my mind, I simply had no other choice.

Once my mother was strong enough to spend the bulk of her day alone, I watched my baby niece Maya a couple of days a week. Having become a caregiver two times over—me, who'd always run from one person and place to the next—blew apart the last vestiges of my independent façade.

Once my mother was well enough to live independently, the various pieces of my life fell into place quickly: within the year, I'd met Ken as well as accepted a position teaching Creative Writing and Business Writing at the University of Colorado Denver. From there, life stormed full steam ahead: Ken and I began planning our wedding, then we bought a car, then a puppy. In this way, I began to form the outlines of my new life, all with the clear knowledge that my mother lived only a few minutes away; Marko and Leslie, just down the road.

Even then, something larger appeared to be at work. Boulder had always been Marko's town, the place where he and

Leslie had gone to college, and it was the one place I never imagined myself living. And yet in the span of a few, short months, it was where I'd met my spouse and landed an academic job.

Apparently, Boulder was where I was supposed to be. Living in the same town as my family would cut me to the quick, as well as teach me life's most important lessons. It was where I would finally grow up.

CHAPTER 6

RETREAT

February continued to be cold and dark. More than anything, I wanted to hole up and hide, let the waves of grief carry me away. Until what? Until spring came or a miracle occurred, I supposed. But I was a mother now, and I had responsibilities. There were only so many things I could push onto the back burner, and feeding my children wasn't among them.

This provided me with a respite from the drudgery of my days as well as made me resentful as hell. As unfair as it seemed, I wanted Ken to do everything so that I could basically disappear. Since he worked from home in the basement, Ken was often underfoot but unavailable, and it drove me batty to always be the one on deck with the kids. I had a sitter so that I could work a few hours a week, but the worse I felt, the less I accomplished. My various responsibilities felt like a noose around my neck, and I often rebelled by taking my unhappiness out on my husband.

Despite all that, I was putting a ridiculous amount of time into our nightly meals. I felt like a slave to my kitchen, shopping and cooking and then cleaning it all up, day after day after day.

I seemed to be driven by demons; if I couldn't be fully present for my children, then at least I could cook for them. So that was what I did, digging out my mother's old recipes and making them from scratch, over and over again.

I missed that old Serbian comfort food, and I went to extraordinary lengths to recreate it. One afternoon, I spent hours looking for a website where I could buy whole pickled cabbage heads so that I could make *sarma*, the minced meat and rice dish that my mother had requested as she was dying. I even considered pickling the cabbage myself, but the instructions were so labor and time-intensive that I eventually moved on to some of my mother's simpler recipes. I made vats of the sweet spaghetti sauce I'd loved as a kid and giant bowls of *kupus*, coleslaw with an oil and vinegar dressing.

And I stepped up my coffee intake. When Ken didn't want any afternoon coffee, I badgered him until he gave in. Just a sip, I said. It's half-decaf!

It pained me beyond measure to be drinking my afternoon coffee alone. Afternoon coffee, I firmly believed, was meant to be shared, and every time I drank it alone, I felt a tiny bit less connected to my Serbian heritage. Every time I drank my coffee alone, my mother slipped away a bit more.

It would take me a full year before I understood that my cooking was another attempt to reconnect with my mother. Food had always been one of my deepest links to my mother, and by obsessing over her old recipes, a part of me was trying to recreate my childhood. Because even though my mother hadn't been emotionally available, she'd always cooked dinners from scratch. Just the aroma of sautéing onions was enough to make me miss her.

No wonder I was cooking like such a madwoman. I was looking for my mother in the only place I knew where to find her.

Like most parent-children relationships, my mother and I often got under each other's skin. Extended periods of time together ended with bickering, one of us lashing out at the other before withdrawing. Both of us craving a connection that seemed impossible to achieve.

Some days, I wondered if the tension between us stemmed from the fact that we were too alike. My mother was always telling me to be less sensitive, not to take things so personally, not to care—even though she cared deeply. Like other immigrant parents, she wanted the best for her children, and what better way to achieve that than to toughen me up. If she made me bulletproof, I wouldn't have to suffer, as she had.

This translated into a low-level, near-constant criticism that I interpreted as rejection. After all, she wanted me to be strong, better than her in all ways. To protect my open and tender heart in ways she never could.

Meanwhile, all I wanted was to be myself, but that person didn't seem to be good enough. So I just tried harder.

I always tried harder.

We had our good times, too, of course. My mother instilled a deep love of literature and the arts within me and Marko, and often encouraged us to think for ourselves. She had a sharp intellect, a wicked sense of humor and a deeply seated rebellious streak; she was a five-foot, five-inch beauty with a sharp nose and Eastern-European accent. Under different circumstances, she would have made an excellent literary critic. When Marko was around, the three of us often laughed to the point of tears.

When it was just the two of us, though, I couldn't seem to get close. I didn't have Marko's gift with levity, and by the time I was an adult, my more serious and intense nature had taken its toll on our relationship. My mother wanted peace while I wanted connection; for years, we weren't able to bridge that gap. She wanted to talk about the news or a house she'd seen on her walk while I wanted to talk about the past or some real-life struggle. In essence, I wanted a mother with whom I could speak freely, someone who could handle my anger, my passion, my insistence on truth—*all* of me.

It would take me years to learn that true intimacy doesn't thrive on discord and defiance. Peace can be just as holy a path to love.

Each day, after dropping Gabriel off at preschool, I sank back into my awful new Grieving with Children life. Despite Ken's colitis, I firmly believed he could watch out for himself. But Gabriel and Nico were only four- and six-years old, far too young for me to mentally check out and raise themselves. Some days, I wished I could just crawl into bed and disappear. Other days, I was so incredibly thankful to have my children tethering me to the ground.

Months would pass before I'd understand this desire to hole up—or, as I thought of it at the time, self-destruct. I was in a giant transition phase, moving from the person I'd once been to the person I would become.

So, much like a caterpillar on the verge of metamorphosis, I found myself withdrawing from the world as I constructed a cocoon around myself. As I understand it, a butterfly is the only animal that completely breaks down and reorders its DNA as it transforms. While it's in a cocoon, it's literally mush. The insect that comes out of the cocoon is a completely different insect from the one that went into it.

This appealed to me on multiple levels. I yearned for the space and time to withdraw from the outside world in order to rebuild myself. Instead, I found myself mired in the details of daily life, with school drop-offs, pick-ups and meal preparation constantly tearing me from my cocoon. Some days, every inter-action with the world felt like it was ripping me wide open; other days I could go out and be "on" for two or three hours before shutting down from the effort.

In some ways, self-destructing would have been a quicker way to have bid farewell to my old self. At least it would have been more familiar—it was what I'd done after my father died, when I quit my promising white-collar publishing sales job to return to tending bar.

I began to wonder if people had midlife affairs or divorced during times of crisis in order to create this transformational space. If I'd had a weaker marriage, I might have run away, es-pecially if I hadn't had children.

Instead, I constantly battled the urge to escape. I fantasized about creating cabins where mourners could be fed and sup-ported for periods of time, much like an artist's community. A week's worth of solitude and space, with someone else cooking, sounded ideal.

A friend told me how her husband had spent an entire year living in a cabin in the woods by himself after his brother died. I envied this, even though I knew that taking myself away from my children might have been catastrophic.

As much as I wanted to run away, a part of me was terrified that doing so would result in the loss of everything and everyone I loved. I'd already lost most of my 20s to grief after my father died, and I was terrified that I was going to lose my 40s as well. And so I remained stuck in this painful limbo, completely forgetting that I alone could let myself out of this prison.

Meanwhile, Marko and I continued our debate about selling the condo. He was itching to get it off his plate, while I couldn't bear to let it go. The condo was all I had left of my mother.

To Marko, the condo was one more estate task that needed to be completed on an already long list. He didn't visit the condo to be close to my mom, like I did. He went to the cemetery, whereas I rarely did. Her grave was just a plot to me; I didn't feel her energy there, as I did in the condo.

Back and forth we went. I guessed that Marko's desire to sell the condo was a way of tamping down his grief, but I wasn't really sure. Our conversations were so filled with logistics that we rarely communicated about our grief. Besides, who was I to say that my process was better? I wasn't even ready to part with my mother's things. We both had our own way of dealing with grief, and I needed to respect that.

Eventually, we decided we would sell the condo in May. I wanted to hold off until the end of summer, but Marko wanted to get the condo on the market at the height of the season, to make sure it sold.

The hospital bills, meanwhile, were slowly becoming more manageable. Boulder Community Hospital had paid the bulk of my mother's bills after receiving the CICP paperwork from CU Anschutz. When they'd balked over some new limitations, Marko had brought in an additional round of supporting paperwork and argued with the powers that be until they finally backed off. Despite our rocky moments, we'd turned out to be a good team. Marko liked doing the physical, out-in-the-world tasks my mother's estate required, while I preferred the ones I could handle from home.

And still, random bills continued to arrive from providers and services I barely remembered. Simply seeing the amount of bills generated by my mother's two-month-long illness was incredible. How the hell did families recover from the financial destruction of sicknesses that were much longer?

Over the course of a few weeks, I noticed an inordinate amount of friends and acquaintances complaining to me about their mothers. On a good day, their complaints struck me as trivial. On a bad day, they infuriated me. How *dare* these women complain to me about their mothers when I'd just lost mine?

Didn't they realize how much their words hurt me? Or had they just forgotten about my loss? My mother had died over two months ago—a lifetime for regular people. But I no longer lived in that world—I lived in a parallel one they couldn't see or understand. Meaning they couldn't see me.

To protect myself, I began to distance myself from these people. Getting through the day was hard enough, and I simply didn't have the energy to educate others on what I needed.

Around this time, I found myself revisiting the painful period after my father's death with new eyes. For a long time, I was ashamed at how long I'd allowed myself to wallow after he died. Everyone thought I'd thrown my life overboard when I left a publishing job selling textbooks to colleges and universities to return to bartending, and for a long time, I'd let this color my interpretation of myself. For nearly five years after my father died, I did little more than work, write and party with my night-owl friends. Instead of giving myself credit for the healing I was doing during that time, I often looked at that period with eyes thickened in shame.

Now I can't help but wonder if that period was simply the necessary order of things—a fallow season. Deep within, shoots and tendrils were beginning to form, though I couldn't yet see them.

My friend Monica had parents in their 80s with myriad health issues. Like me, she'd been through countless health scares and ICU drills. More than most, she understood the depth of my loss, and it terrified her.

"I've been trying to prepare for when my parents die," she said one day. "If I feel it now, maybe it won't be so hard when my mother dies."

I shook my head. "I'd felt that way, too," I said. "But the fear's a waste of time, because it doesn't actually prepare you for her death. All it does is rob you of the time you have left.

"Spend more time with her instead," I urged. "Once she's gone, you can never get that time back."

During this dark, late-winter period after my mother's death, Nico and Gabriel continued to be my lifeline. Most mornings, they were the only thing that got me up and going. At bedtime, I hugged them tight, thankful they still wanted me to put them to sleep.

My emotions were unstable as hell, and I spent many days in a state of anger, wishing someone would take care of me. And yet for the life of me, I couldn't reach out and ask for help. Most people assumed I was doing better now that a couple of months had passed, not worse, and I didn't have the heart to tell them otherwise. Doing so felt like failure.

On the few occasions I'd tried, many people had responded with discomfort. Others simply changed the topic, which felt like a giant slap in the face.

After that had happened a few times, it took all of my courage to even test the waters, sharing bits and pieces with the few friends I thought could handle it. Even then, I never allowed myself to fully admit the depth of my grief. It didn't feel safe, and I didn't know what I'd do if I lost those friends, too. So I kept up a partial wall between us, even as I worked to break it down, one brick at a time.

The only two people I felt like I could really lean on were Ken and Arielle, my therapist, and I leaned on them heavily. Despite the distance between us, Ken was my lifeline—the person I turned to when I desperately needed a hug, the person I relied on to take Nico and Gabriel when I was about to snap.

Despite the old resentments that arose for us during times of crisis, we were starting to find small, concrete ways to help each other, like me letting Ken sleep in on weekends to combat his colitis, and Ken taking the kids on Friday nights, when I was fried from the week.

In between these bits and pieces of kindness, we continued to lick our wounds—each wishing for the kind of space and support that no longer existed in a marriage with young, needy children.

In this way, we limped along, barely recognizing this blooming new bud on our relationship for the miracle it was. Ever so slowly, we were learning how to be there for each other while also taking care of ourselves. Give and receive, give and receive. This was the mantra that would finally save us.

One afternoon, Arielle told me that most people are lucky if they have one or two people they can really count on in their grief.

I was stunned.

"*One or two people?*" I said. "Are you kidding me?"

She shook her head.

So this, too, was normal. I wasn't the only person who felt alone and abandoned in her grief. For months, I'd felt that most people weren't willing to touch my grief with a 10-foot pole.

Even worse was the invisible hierarchy of grief that I encountered at nearly every turn. The suggestion that my loss wasn't really a loss because it was only my mother and heck, we all expect our parents to die. It wasn't like I'd lost my spouse, you know. It wasn't my *child*.

But I wasn't trying to compare my loss with anyone else's; I wasn't trying to compete. And I sure as hell wasn't trying to take away someone else's grief by sharing mine. All I wanted was someone to acknowledge my grief. To say, *Hey, I see you. I get it. And man, does this suck.*

I was so damn tired of all the judgment and advice. All I wanted was empathy, not people telling me to buck up and get over it; my mother had had a good life, yadda yadda. My grief was *my* grief, and no one had the right to take that away from me.

Besides, I wasn't only grieving my mother—I was grieving the loss of both of my parents, the family foundation that no longer existed. That alone was a huge identity shift, and it infuriated me to have people who hadn't experienced such a loss judging my journey.

Thankfully, I had books to keep me company. Books like Alexander Levy's *The Orphaned Adult* that validated my identity shift. Books that showed me my grief wasn't just real, it was *normal.* Books that reinforced my belief that stuffing feelings often leads to disastrous effects years later, such as midlife crises and divorce.

As for the friends and acquaintances in my life, it wasn't long before I shut down and stopped reaching out almost entirely. Fuck it, I thought. I'd get through this grief thing by myself.

All I needed was Ken. And Arielle. And Nico and Gabriel. And my dog.

Boy, did I sound pathetic. I sounded just like Steve Martin in the movie *The Jerk* after Bernadette Peters leaves him:

> *Well, I'm gonna go then. And I don't need any of this. I don't need this stuff, and I don't need you. And that's it and that's the only thing I need, is this. I don't need this or*

this. Just this ashtray. And this paddle game and that's all I
need. And this remote control. The ashtray, the paddle
game, and the remote control, that's all I need ...

Meanwhile, I found myself obsessing over the grief culture in
America—or, more to the point, the lack thereof. As far as I
could tell, we no longer had any kind of communal container
for grief beyond the funeral and memorial process. Our con-
sumerist society seemed to have swallowed that up as well. How
had we ended up so backwards, I wondered, worshipping work,
busyness and material goods over our relationships with each
other? Especially when love and connection are the barometers
most of us will use to measure our lives on our deathbeds, at
least according to Bronnie Ware's book, *The Top Five Regrets of
the Dying*.

Worse still, I knew from personal experience that grief *could*
be communal, that mourners didn't have to suffer alone. Childhood summers in the former Yugoslavia during the 70s had
taught me that. Back then, when someone died, the community
rallied around the deceased's family, bringing food, comfort and
support. Visible reminders of their grief surrounded the be-
reaved, from mourning black attire to mirrors covered with
black cloth. Music ceased for an extended period of time, while
traditional church services were held on the third day, ninth day
and 40th days as well as at three months, six months, nine
months and one year.

Such rituals created a container for the family's grief. Not
only was their loss reflected in the eyes of their community, but
it was *accepted*. Death and grief were recognized as normal stages
in life, and mourners didn't have to traverse this barren land

alone. Instead, such rituals allowed them to be held by their community in their grief.

Very few of us have this luxury in the United States today. The Jewish community maintains shiva, a week-long communal mourning ritual that's followed by modified periods of 30-day and one-year mourning, and I can't tell you how much this ritual called to me. But I couldn't simply usurp another heritage's rituals, much as I would have liked. I needed my own.

And yet, it didn't feel quite right to follow the cultural traditions from my Yugoslav childhood, either. Those belonged to another time and place, certainly not the bright, sunny Colorado life I now inhabited. A simple ritual like covering the mirrors probably would have terrified my children.

Despite that, black mourning attire called to me on a deep level. I craved a physical symbol of my grief, if only for logistical ease. School drop-offs and pick-ups might have been easier if others understood I was mourning, as would chores like shopping for groceries—all of which had become treacherous caverns to be crossed since I'd lost my mother.

As it was, I had to contend with numerous painful interactions, such as the acquaintance who'd asked about our winter break when school started back up after the holidays. Did I tell her the truth—that I'd buried my mother and it was terrible? Or did I mumble an unintelligible answer before suffering through her holiday story?

Such interactions tore me to shreds, and I had to navigate them on a daily basis. As such, I dreaded going out into public and often put errands on an endless back burner. But the one thing I couldn't put on the back burner was dropping off and picking up my kids, and since Gabriel was still in preschool, this meant *four* school drop-offs and pick-ups a day. The pressure of so much social interaction nearly drove me insane, and I often found myself desperately wishing for some kind of outward mark so that others could understand my grief. A Scarlet letter, perhaps, but in black—a symbol created out of compassion instead of shame.

So I took to the Internet to see what kinds of kind of current, accepted mourning rituals existed in the U.S. Besides traditional funerals, receptions and celebrations of life, I didn't find much. What I did find, however, were hundreds of community boards on the topic. Many others also wished black mourning attire still existed. I combed through hundreds of posts from people who were searching for the old-fashioned, clear-cut mourning rituals they remembered from their youth, just like me.

Those rituals, I learned, slowly disappeared in the West during the 20th century as women began working outside the home, and war increased the number of our dead. Instead of washing and dressing the body by ourselves in our homes, hospitals took over this intimate task, further isolating us from death in the process. Bit by bit, the connection between private grief and public mourning began to diminish, until it all but disappeared.

These days, the public face of mourning in the West tends to revolve around celebrity deaths. The communal grief that arises from such events serves to fulfill the need of the larger community—meaning that we're also processing our own grief as we're crying over the death of Princess Diana or Muhammad Ali. In a similar vein, communal losses such as 9/11 and the Sandy Hook shooting serve as public receptacles for our grief.

My brief education in public mourning fascinated as well as disturbed me, and I found myself thinking about how differently my mother's final days might have been if she'd declined naturally, at home. Instead, she'd spent the last week of her life in a brutal nose-dive after her doctors subjected her to that god-awful, last-ditch chemo effort in the hospital. By the time we were able to bring her home through hospice, she only lived a few more hours. Perhaps my mother's death would have been more humane if she'd been allowed to fully transition at home, without that unnecessary chemo intervention. If nothing else, her death might have felt more honest.

In early March, I woke up with an intense urge to cut off my long hair. That would provide a clear physical marker, I thought. Show the world that I was no longer the person I'd once been. But there was only one problem with my new plan: I didn't like myself with short hair.

So I fought the urge for weeks, despite its increasing intensity. I had to keep reminding myself how miserable I was when I transitioned from shoulder-length hair to an inch-long pixie cut right after Nico's first birthday. That, too, had marked another giant transition in my life—my emergence as a new mother. At the time, I'd wanted some kind of symbolic marker to show that I'd survived my first year of motherhood. But as soon as I cut off all my hair, I hated it.

Nope. I wasn't making *that* mistake again.

So I kept searching, trying to figure out what kind of physical change I could make. All the while, the urge to cut off my hair continued to scratch away at me like a giant itch. I wanted—*ached*—for some kind of stark physical marker to embody my loss. At one point, I realized that this might be why some people scar themselves, to have an outward marker of their pain.

I turned to jewelry next, and found multiple online websites selling modern replicas of Victorian mourning jewelry. Other sites offered religious jewelry that didn't resonate with me. Neither did the memorial jewelry I came across (although I learned you can memorialize your loved one's ashes into a necklace or ring). I also found quite a bit of sentimental dove and butterfly jewelry, none of which resonated with me, either.

Wasn't there anything more contemporary? Much of the jewelry I found seemed aimed at an older crowd. But what about younger folks who'd suffered a loss? Wasn't there anything available for us?

Eventually, I remembered that Meghan O'Rourke, author of *The Long Goodbye*, had bought a black and white friendship bracelet as a personal marker of her loss after her mother died. She didn't take it off for three months.

Of course. A bracelet—something small and unobtrusive, something just for me—it was perfect! I could share it if I wanted to, or hide it if I didn't.

And just like that, the purpose of my mourning symbol shifted. Instead of black mourning attire that announced my grieving status to everyone I met, a bracelet could be just for me—a way of honoring myself. By wearing such a real and tangible symbol of my grief, I'd be giving myself permission to *feel* that grief. And after having hidden so much of my grief from the world around me, I needed permission.

One afternoon, I was in Nico's first-grade classroom, sorting and filling the folders that went home with the kids every Friday. After having handed off this volunteer chore for the past few months, it felt a bit surreal to be back in the classroom. The kids were out on the playground, where life stopped for no one, and I was beyond thankful that I'd chosen such a simple, no-stress volunteer job for the year. To have been among the kids for even a full hour would have clobbered me.

I was sitting in a blue, plastic first-grader's chair, coffee in hand, when I came across a paper with Nico's name on it. I bent closer. The assignment was called "Small Moments," with "Seed Stories" as the subtitle. The rest of the paper was a drawing of a giant slice of watermelon.

The words "Big Story Idea" were written in the middle of the watermelon, which had been filled in with red crayon. Beneath that, Nico had written "A Seremony."

I stared at the paper in surprise. A ceremony.

Beneath "A Seremony" were six giant seeds filled with my child's beautiful, first-grade handwriting:

> *I wore my suit.*
> *We got cadols [candles].*
> *We ate a varity [variety] of food.*
> *There were three priests.*
> *The chirch [church] was Srbon [Serbian].*
> *We all drest [dressed] nice.*

But the real kicker was the "bite" taken out of the watermelon, where my son had written, "it was fun."

Fun? Nico thought that the 40th day memorial service at my mother's church had been fun? Not only had he barely mentioned the ceremony, but at certain points, he'd acted like he

104

didn't want to be there. I had no idea the day had impacted him so much.

When I asked Nico about the assignment later, he shrugged it off. Sure, he said, the ceremony was fun. But he didn't want to talk about it, and I didn't press. Instead, I asked if I could keep the paper for myself. He liked that, so I added the Seed Stories to the small, informal altar that I'd started for my mother in my office, where it would remain one of my most prized possessions.

Later that night, as we were in bed reading, I asked Nico if he had any questions about church. It felt strange to realize I'd never really talked with him about God or religion.

"Why don't we go to church?" he asked.

"Well," I hedged. "Daddy and I grew up in different churches, and neither one really fits our beliefs today."

"What does that mean?"

I took a deep breath. "Most religions teach that you have to go to church if you want to talk to God. I don't believe that," I said. "I believe that God is all around us, everywhere, and that we can communicate with him by ourselves, that we don't need a church or a priest to help us do that."

He thought about that for a moment. "God's all around us?"

I nodded. "And he's also a part of us. Just like he's a part of everything in this world."

Nico thought about that for a while. "So then how do you talk to him?"

"Well, sometimes I go outside. I believe God is everywhere in nature, and that's one reason it feels so good to be outside." I paused. "I also talk to him by praying."

"How do you pray?"

"Well, different people pray differently, but I can show you how I pray."

Nico liked that idea, so I once again showed him how we crossed ourselves in the Serbian Orthodox tradition, with three fingers pressed together; in the name of the Father, the Son and the Holy Spirit. Amen.

We practiced this a few times. It was tricky to get your fingers right.

"Then I usually ask God to protect my family and the people I love," I said. "You can do it anyway you like. Just say whatever makes sense to you."

Nico sat up excitedly. "Like this? Dear God, please bless …"

I listened while he went on and on, asking God to bless his family, his friends, his toys, his stuffed animals, etc. He was very specific, so it took awhile. I listened with a full heart: I'd prayed exactly like him when I was a kid, often falling asleep before I finished my prayer.

These days, no one knew I still prayed—not even Ken. To hear Nico praying exactly as I'd prayed as a child was uncanny, and it felt like another small pebble of proof that there was a hell of a lot more to this crazy life than ever meets the eye.

CHAPTER 7

THREE DREAMS

Over the course of one week, I had three intense dreams about my mom. In the first dream, my mother was driving around a crowded parking lot while I ran around, trying to get closer. But no matter how hard I tried, I couldn't get close to her. It was excruciating. Then the dream morphed and my mother and I were ambling through an indoor walking mall from the 70s. She was walking with a cane, and we eventually sat down in an empty, ugly little café and had coffee.

In the second dream, we were in a blindingly white, two-bedroom apartment on the top floor of a European building. A family friend who'd spurned my mother in life was visiting my dying mother. The woman was 10-15 years older than in real life, and as she came out of my mother's bedroom, I could see that they'd made their peace.

In the last dream, I was driving at night. It was pitch-black, late, and after a few moments my mother appeared in the car ahead of me. She was sitting in the back window of a station wagon, facing me, smiling. She was glowing and healthy, looking just like she used to before she got sick, wearing her favorite outfit, a maroon sweater over her pink shirt. And that smile!

There she was again, my beautiful mother. She looked so happy.

CHAPTER 8

RED

When my mom was dying, the oncologist recommended undergoing early, regular colonoscopies because of my family history. As if that was just what I wanted to hear as my mother was dying, that my parents' illnesses meant I might die early, too, *thank you.* Then my OB started in on me. By the time my regular doctor added his voice to the chorus, I'd had enough of their talk. Especially since the CU Anschutz oncology specialist we'd visited had informed me and Marko that my mother's cancer was extremely rare, and posed no risk whatsoever for our families.

Despite that, their words continued to wear away at me until I finally scheduled a consult with a gastroenterologist. I wasn't as afraid of colon cancer as I was of the colonoscopy itself. After my mother went into septic shock when her colon was punctured, I was terrified I was going to die on the table, the victim of another terrible mistake.

So I handled that by going overboard in choosing a doctor. I wasn't fond of the GI doctors Ken saw for his ulcerative colitis, so I looked for someone new. I wanted to be sure that I could trust this new doctor—and to do that, I wanted to be able to look him in the face.

To me, this seemed like a sensible approach, but it wasn't to the gastroenterologist. Apparently, only patients with existing GI problems make appointments for consults before a colonoscopy. As he let me know from the moment I walked into his office.

He was pissed off and grumpy from the start, and kept asking why I'd scheduled a consult. I told him about my family history, but that didn't seem to matter. Was there anything wrong with me? he wanted to know. Otherwise, this appointment was a waste of his time.

I was stunned by his sheer and utter rudeness, and figured he'd back down once he got that off his chest. But he kept on.

"I don't know why you're here," he said, "if there's *nothing wrong with you.*"

"With my family history," I repeated, "it was important for me to meet you."

He sighed dramatically. "Hop on the table," he said, "so that I can *examine* you."

I climbed onto the table, pissed off beyond belief. My chest and my throat had constricted into a tight, painful ball, and I was doing my damnedest to just get through the appointment without making things worse.

He picked up his stethoscope and held it to my chest. "Even though you have no *symptoms* and there's nothing *wrong* with you."

I couldn't believe what an ass he was being, and it sucked to high heaven to be in such a physically vulnerable position when I wanted to punch him in the face. The "examination" was a sham, and as he pretended to listen to my heartbeat, my breath became more and more shallow. Despite my best efforts to stop them, tears were starting to leak from my eyes.

There would be no getting through this, I realized. So I took a depth breath and wiped my cheeks with the back of my hand. "My mother went septic from a doctor who punctured her colon," I said shakily. "I wanted to meet you before the colonoscopy to make sure I could trust you. That's all I asked for—just to *meet* you. You didn't have to be such a jerk."

The doctor exhaled, suddenly, deflated. He dropped his stethoscope and looked at me—really looked at me for the first time during our appointment.

"Look," he said. "I'm sorry about your mother. But it's extremely rare for a gastroenterologist to puncture a colon. I've done thousands of colonoscopies in my career and I've only had one perforation. If I met with every patient before their procedure, I'd be out of business."

"That's not *my* problem," I said.

"You're right, it's not."

He rubbed his face with his hands. "Well, we can't work together now. The patient-doctor relationship is fucked—excuse my language—and we won't be able to regain that integrity."

I nodded. Agreed, asshole.

He pulled out his prescription pad. "Normally, the consult has to be followed by a procedure with the same doctor, but I'll contact another doctor and explain what happened so he'll take you. Do you have anyone you prefer?"

I gave him the name of the doctor I wish I'd chosen in the first place, and we retreated into our separate corners.

I was still shaky and pissed off when I left his office, but also proud that I'd stood up for myself. Maybe, just maybe, I'd taught that asshole something about relating to his patients.

For weeks, I'd been drawn to the color red, wearing it whenever I could, almost as if my lifeblood was starting to creep back in. The color was vibrant, passionate and highly symbolic of how I wanted to live my life, with no holding back. I was tired of living a half-ass life, hiding who I really was in order to not rock the boat.

Eventually, this translated into deciding to dye a small section of my hair red. Adding a red streak felt fun and powerful, a small beginning to a new chapter. Plus, it would help fulfill the outer change I'd been seeking, act as a stark physical marker I could easily change once it no longer suited me.

My hairdresser Amy, who'd seen me through the short-hair debacle that accompanied new motherhood, loved the idea, and I left our appointment with a six-inch streak of bright *Run Lola Run* red hanging down my left shoulder. I felt more like myself almost immediately. Rebellious, and free.

My friends loved it, as did Ken and the kids. Others didn't mention it, and I assumed this meant they didn't care for it. That was OK. The red streak wasn't for them, after all; it was for me. A symbol of my newfound freedom.

The red streak was helping me break out of my shell in more ways than one. Every time I looked in the mirror, I was reminded of the .true person I was—not the small, timid person I'd become.

So I began taking small, calculated risks, challenging myself in bits and pieces. I went to my book group instead of bailing at the last minute. Talked to a friendly mother at pick-up. Smiled at the grocery store cashier. Made eye contact when I wanted to run away.

Bit by bit, I waded in deeper. When friends from my dance class asked how I was, I challenged myself to answer somewhat truthfully. I did the same with friends. Sometimes I'd hint it was a hard day, and other times I'd come right out and say it.

In this way, I tested the waters. I wanted to know who could handle my grief, and who couldn't. As far as I was concerned, the people who couldn't handle my grief couldn't handle *me*. My grief had made me into the person I now was, and I was no longer interested in being with people who wanted the old me. She no longer existed.

Even though the red streak had fulfilled part of the physical change I was seeking, I was still searching for a suitable mourning bracelet. I wanted to find something that might help others as well as myself. So for weeks, I'd been scouring the Internet, looking at silver bracelets, beaded bracelets and bracelets made of semiprecious gemstones. Nothing felt right.

Then, one afternoon as my niece Maya was making Nico and Gabriel plastic wristbands with a Rainbow Loom, it hit me. A black silicone rubber version of the iconic Livestrong wristband—of course! Something that could work for men or women of all ages, as well as teens and children. Something simple, yet meaningful that could serve as a physical marker of the grief moving inside of us.

I spent the next few weeks ordering silicone rubber bracelet samples from various companies, testing for quality and viability. Each bracelet arrived with a different word or symbol etched into the band as I tested different phrases, trying to decipher what would be most meaningful.

Bit by bit, I was growing closer with one of the mothers at Gabriel's preschool. Jess was a kind, thoughtful, down-to-earth person who'd already been down the grief road with her husband after his brother and father had died. Meaning she got it. She understood what grief looked like in real time and she wasn't afraid of it.

She knew that I wasn't over my loss even when I didn't mention it, and she wasn't afraid to ask me how I was *really* doing. Unlike so many others, she didn't change the topic when I answered honestly, and could handle my sadness without having to try to fix it.

This was such a gift that for a long time I hardly dared trust it. As the months wore on, we grew closer and closer, and our new friendship blossomed.

For months, I'd been aching for a beach vacation. Grief was exhausting. The months leading up to my mother's death had also taken their toll as I'd juggled her declining health with the needs of my children, and the only thing I wanted was to hit a beach and camp out on the sand for weeks.

Spring Break was right around the corner, but we couldn't afford a beach vacation, so Ken and I decided to take the kids to the YMCA in Estes Park for a long weekend instead. It was close and cheap, and at least we'd still be getting out of town.

That felt like a good compromise until we arrived at the YMCA. How had I forgotten that Estes Park had been my mother's favorite place? For years, we'd marked her birthday with a family weekend at the YMCA, and her ghost was everywhere I looked.

To make matters worse, my 43rd birthday landed on the final day of our trip. By the time my birthday rolled around, I was a mess. It was my first birthday without my mother, and the knowledge that there would be no call from her, no message, no nothing, was just too much.

When Ken had asked what I wanted to do for my birthday, I'd told him I didn't want to do anything. I didn't want to invite friends to any kind of celebration; I didn't even want a cake. I just wanted the day to pass unmarked. But now that my birthday had arrived, that was the last thing I wanted. Even though I was spending the day with Ken and the kids, I felt deeply alone—nearly inconsolable—and I realized what a giant mistake it had been, coming up to Estes. What the hell had I been thinking?

Arielle helped me shed some light on the weekend during our next appointment. Anniversaries, holidays and birthdays, I learned, bring up fresh waves of grief because they're clear reminders of our loss. During such days, we feel the absence of our beloved that much more strongly. Because—of course—my mother was always there on my birthday. Even if she wasn't, she'd call. Send a card. And now there was nothing. Just incredible, open gaping silence where she should have been.

That alone was painful enough. But Arielle helped me see that I was leaning on my mother's old patterns as a way of reconnecting with her. Isolating myself, criticizing myself—they were old, ingrained patterns I'd learned from my mother, the default mindset I fell into when I missed her most.

Except that that default mindset just created more suffering for me and my family. Wasn't it time, Arielle suggested, that I found a new way to connect with my mother?

As the dust from my birthday began to settle, I dug back into my work on the mourning bracelets. I still ached for an outward symbol of my grief, especially after the Spring Break debacle, and from my online research, I knew I wasn't alone in this feeling. So I decided to move ahead and create a wristband that might benefit us all.

After a few more weeks of trial and error, I found a high-quality wristband and embedded the word "Remember" into the silicone band. Remember your loved one. Remember your grief. Remember your loss. Remember. Don't let the world teach you to forget.

When the "Remember" wristband arrived, I slipped it onto my wrist and didn't take it off. Later that night, I took a deep breath and ordered 1000 more. I'd reached out to a friend to help me create a simple website where I could sell the bands, and I was excited beyond belief. Finally, something I could *do* with my grief, something tangible. I wanted to help as many people as I could.

If my birthday wasn't hard enough, Mother's Day just about killed me. I found myself getting grumpier and grumpier as the day edged closer. Thankfully, I rarely watched TV, so I didn't have to deal with the Mother's Day commercials.

Even so, I couldn't escape the holiday. Mother's Day was splashed all over the newspaper ads, and every trip to Target was a grim reminder that no, I would not be buying any Mother's Day cards for anyone this year. I found myself irritated beyond belief with Hallmark. Whose stupid idea was this holiday, anyway? Surely, I wasn't the only one dreading it.

And yet I didn't hear a peep from anyone else who was struggling. So I reached out to the few women I knew who'd lost their mothers. My sister-in-law Leslie had lost her mother 20 years ago, but now that so much time had passed, she'd reclaimed the holiday, celebrating it with her daughter, Maya.

My friend Emily, whose mother had died when she was 18, also dreaded the day. Like me, she hated all the build-up. For her, the day was even more complicated, since her mother hadn't lived long enough to see her get married or meet her daughter.

Even though Emily had a different set of holes in her past than I did, it helped to know I wasn't an anomaly for eschewing the day. And even though I was a mother myself, I couldn't celebrate my own motherhood role—not this year, anyway.

After my birthday fiasco, Arielle had suggested incorporating some kind of ritual into the holiday so that I could more consciously remember my mother, but I couldn't think of anything that felt right. I could light a candle, sure. But that wasn't big enough. Important enough. Meaningful enough.

So I twisted and turned when the holiday arrived, glad that Mother's Day was only 24 hours long. The kids gave me a sweet card, and Ken gave me a little gift, both of which I could barely take in. I writhed my way through the hours, waiting for the day to end. Nothing, absolutely nothing, seemed to help.

Our May deadline of selling my mother's condo had come and gone. For weeks, Marko had been steadily emptying the condo while I dragged my feet. I'd stalled long enough, and as much as I wanted to hang on to this last tangible piece of my mother, I knew we needed to get the condo on the market during the high season.

By this point, Marko had put many of the condo's larger items into storage. With the paintings and most of the extraneous furniture gone, I no longer felt my mother's presence. The condo had become just another empty vessel of what once was, and even I knew that it was time to let it go. So Marko and I scheduled an entire weekend devoted to clearing out the rest of the condo at the end of May, before the kids got out of school.

As I was trying to wrap my head around this, Marko was descending into battle with Olga, the cemetery manager. For weeks, she'd been hounding him to finalize my mother's headstone, despite her initial counsel that we had a full year to take care of it.

Instead of acquiescing, Marko pushed back. Choosing a headstone was a bridge we planned on crossing after we sold the condo. Marko and I both wanted a strong, beautiful piece of stonework that symbolized my mother and what she'd stood for, and neither of us wanted to make that decision under duress.

Olga didn't seem to understand that we might need more time. Irritated by her constant barrage, Marko pushed back about the barren state of my mother's grave. Olga had promised to plant grass seed on my mother's grave after the burial, but so far there was nothing but mud.

For weeks, they went round and round in a strange power struggle: headstone, grass, headstone, grass. I watched from the sidelines, fascinated by the weirdness of it all. Olga was an older woman originally from the Czech Republic, with her own son and grandchildren, and I couldn't help but wonder if there was some family pattern or something about our shared Eastern European heritage setting each of them off.

Either way, I didn't get it. I offered to help, but Marko didn't want me involved. Apparently, this one was his battle.

While Marko was rumbling with his ethnic roots in the Olga debacle, mine were slowly slipping away. One warm afternoon, I overheard an acquaintance at the grocery store speaking German with her child. As we chatted, I found myself confessing that I wish I'd spoken more Serbian with my children.

While she encouraged me to "start now," I brushed off her suggestions, wondering why on earth I'd opened up this can of worms. I couldn't say that I'd spoken Serbian with my mom, because then I'd have to say that my mother had died and I couldn't go there with this woman, not right now. So I came up with a host of lame excuses, then went home and berated myself for having gotten into the conversation in the first place.

The truth was, I'd always thought I'd have more time. I'd always planned on teaching my kids Serbian, and figured it would be easy enough to do with my mom's help. What I didn't count on was that we'd speak less Serbian than we did before I had children, partly because Ken didn't understand what we were saying, and partly because parenting had turned out to be so much harder than I'd expected. In those early days of new motherhood, I hadn't had the energy to teach the kids a new language on top of everything else. Maybe once they were finally sleeping, I told myself. Once they were older, more independent ...

And now, here we were.

For weeks, I mulled the language issue over. As the days passed, so did my hope of teaching my children Serbian. The sadder I felt about my mom, the less I was able to accomplish beyond just getting through the day. After a while, the idea of teaching them Serbian began to seem hopeless.

My mood continued to sink, and with it sank whole chunks of my heritage. Without my mother, there was no one at the helm of my Serbian heritage but me. And here I was, married to a Japanese American man, with wholly American kids. What were the chances that my kids would even care about their Serbian heritage when Ken's heritage was the more dominant of the two? After all, they carried Ken's last name, their physical features were part-Asian, they had a giant tree of Japanese American relatives who lived in the U.S. and they could go to Japanese restaurants whenever they wanted.

Meanwhile, my children wore no obvious Serbian features, their Serbian relatives all lived abroad and there were no nearby Serbian restaurants they could visit if they so desired. Perhaps in Chicago or Milwaukee, where there were still Serbian restaurants and large Serbian populations, but in Colorado? In *Boulder*?

My mood sank so low that I even began to question the meaning of my Serbian heritage. A decade ago, I'd been living in Serbia and flirting with the idea of making my move permanent. I'd spent the decade before that writing about my heritage and the collective guilt I felt for belonging to an ethnic group who'd committed some of the worst atrocities since WWII. In short, I'd spent most of my adult life trying to integrate the Serbian and American sides of myself.

Here I was, now, ready to toss that all aside. With my mother gone, my most visceral connection to Serbia had also been severed. Yes, I remained loosely connected to a few relatives on Facebook, but it was rare that anyone beyond my half-brother Miki reached out to us.

In the U.S., it was just me and Marko. To go back to Serbia now would have been like ripping out my heart. I couldn't do it.

When, then, would I?

Could I—ever?

When Miki called on Skype, I told him we were thinking of visiting in another year or two, when the kids got older, but even as I said them the words didn't feel true. And if I didn't introduce my kids to my heritage soon, how long before their connection was also severed? How long until they simply forgot that they were half Serbian?

As for me, my Serbian heritage began to seem like a fight I was done fighting. Hardly anyone in my current life knew how deeply I'd identified with my Serbian heritage, and that made the idea of letting it go that much easier.

One night in bed, I thought, so this is how it happens. This is how we become Americanized, lose all sense of who we are and where we came from. This is how we lose ourselves.

BOOK 3

BECOMING

*I would like to beg you, dear Sir, as well as I can, to
have patience with everything unresolved in your
heart and to try to love the questions themselves as if
they were locked rooms or books written in a very
foreign language. Don't search for the answers, which
could not be given to you now, because you would
not be able to live them. And the point is, to live everything. Live the questions now. Perhaps then, some-
day far in the future, you will gradually, without
even noticing it, live your way into the answer.*

—RAINER MARIA RILKE,
LETTERS TO A YOUNG POET

CHAPTER 9

FIRE

On a bright, sunny Saturday morning at the end of May, Marko and I started the arduous process of dividing up what was left of my mother's things. Marko had opened all the windows of my mother's condo and a cool breeze was blowing through. It was a beautiful, picture-perfect, spring morning, none of which negated the enormity of the task before us.

Thankfully, Marko was prepared. To ease our workload, he'd pulled all of my mother's dishes out of the cabinets and placed them on the counters. He'd done the same with her books and other possessions. The condo looked like a giant estate sale, which made it easier for us to walk through and pick out what we wanted before packing the rest away.

As we moved through the two-bedroom condo, it became clear that Marko and I were a good team, with our different strengths and weaknesses. Thankfully, my mom had never been a material person, and didn't have rooms full of stuff. Her condo was small, neat and fairly easy to manage. Despite that, it was beyond painful to go through her stuff and divvy it up. To streamline the process, we started three categories: keep, donate and deal with later.

As had been the case throughout the entire grieving process, different aspects of the process affected us differently. My mother's favorite coffee cup gave Marko pause while the purple plate from my childhood brought me back. After my mother went back to work, she'd left my afterschool snack in the fridge on that plate, and I could almost see the hunks of cheese and tomato wedges waiting for me, covered in Saran Wrap.

Once we'd whipped through the kitchen, we tackled the spare bedroom. Marko had already taken apart the bookshelf and put everything into stacks, making it easier to scan for books we wanted to keep. I was beyond thankful he'd done so much preparatory work—without those extra steps, I might have easily sunken into overwhelm and short-circuited.

So many books I'd given my mother throughout the years, all those birthday cards and letters. The *Dear Grandma* book I'd bought for her after Nico was born. What in the world was I supposed to do with this stuff? Marko recognized my suffering and compassionately suggested we box up these items, to be dealt with later.

His breaking point, meanwhile, was her closet. I took a deep breath and waded in. The clothes! I stood there for a few minutes, in stupefied shock. They still smelled of my mother, with a hint of her perfume. I took a deep breath and got busy, saving some of her favorite clothes, items that reminded me of better times. The pink shirt she wore on special occasions, the one that made her face light up. The comfy maroon jacket I'd given her that she loved. Her colors, the memory of her smiling in these clothes, laughing. It was too much. It was just brutal.

After I'd put the obvious items into the donation pile, I stuffed the rest into a go-through-later bag. Marko didn't want any of the clothes, but I craved them, somehow. In some way, this was the closest I could get to my mother—to hold her red sweatshirt close to my cheek, inhale her scent, the faint lingering mix of laundry detergent, shampoo, *her*.

My mother. How could this be all I had left?

By the following afternoon, we'd finished clearing out the condo and had transported my mother's burgundy couches into my basement. As the afternoon deepened, Marko and I stacked what was left of my mother's furniture into a giant puzzle piece in the parking lot. As we were finishing, it started to drizzle. A truck for the hospice donation program we'd chosen would pick it up in the morning.

The condo was finally empty. The puzzle-shaped furniture was all we had left. Sitting there in the rain, it looked so sad and empty that I took a photo as a way of memorializing it.

So this was what a life came down to, I thought, a few over-sized pieces of furniture piled into an empty parking lot. I couldn't stop looking at it, even after I'd climbed into my car. Marko had driven away before me, and as I watched the sun starting to set, my heart went with it. It was a quiet Sunday night, with no one else out and about. It felt like the last day on earth.

A new emptiness moved in after the condo was gone. The only tangible evidence of my mother's life now resided in my basement and garage. My mother. Where *was* she?

Within days, Marko had placed the condo was on the market. Because of the Affordable Housing program rules, we had to sell the condo through the same program. This translated into an open house followed by a lottery for interested bidders. Once the winner was chosen, she was allowed to put in an offer. After we'd accepted the buyer's offer and were starting to feel as if we might be done with this piece of my mother's estate, Marko called in a panic.

There had been a fire at my mother's condo. Wait. No, there *was* a fire at my mom's condo. *Right now.*

He and his family had been out for a bike ride when they saw fire trucks close to my mother's home. As they pedaled closer, they found that the source of the fire was another condo in my mother's building. Although the fire had been nearly extinguished, there was no telling how much damage my mother's unit had sustained. Firemen had broken down her door and there appeared to be smoke and water damage.

"I knew we should have sold it earlier!" Marko said.

Once we were better able to ascertain the night's events, we learned that the damage wasn't as bad as we'd anticipated. Since my mother's condo had been two units down from the fire, there had been smoke damage, but no water damage.

Marko and I spent the next few days high on adrenaline, researching smoke mitigation companies so that we could began the repair process. Even though we were thankful that the damage hadn't been worse, it felt like the gods were fucking with us, taunting us by showing us we weren't rid of the condo, *not yet.* Ha, ha, you silly humans! You think you're in charge? You've got another thing coming.

Meanwhile, Olga had started agitating again. You need to finish the headstone, she insisted to my brother, *now*. Over and over again, she launched the same missive. Marko upped his counterattack, insisting on grass. She'd promised countless times that the grave would be covered in grass by spring. It was already June. Where was the grass?

I tried to step in and downplay everything with some finely-worded emails, to no avail. No matter what I did or said, Olga insisted on communicating with Marko only. Clearly, this was their war.

About the only thing I could help with was research. Marko and I had decided we wanted to etch a hawk onto the back of my mother's headstone, but we couldn't find the right image. So I kept looking.

CHAPTER 10

BREATHE

One early morning at the end of June, Ken drove me to my first-ever colonoscopy. I was terrified, doing my best to trust that everything would be OK and that the doctor wouldn't puncture my colon, sending me into septic shock, like my mother.

Ken stayed with the kids while the nurse checked me in and began the initial steps of the outpatient process. After they left, I felt so damn alone. So I started talking, as I often do when I'm nervous, attempting to connect with the nurse and anesthesiologist. With any luck, they'd realize I was an actual human being, not just a patient. This was my wild card. Getting the doctor and the techs to see that I was a real person was the only way I could think of to positively influence the outcome.

The anesthesiologist gave me Fentanyl, a powerful opioid used for conscious sedation, and the next thing I knew, I was groggily waking up to hear my new gastroenterologist—a man who actually smiled, thank God—telling me I was as healthy as could be.

How to explain the relief that washed over me once I'd left the recovery room and the nurse wheeled me out to the car? I looked at my husband and children, feeling a deep glimmer of hope—not only had I survived my colonoscopy, but I was healthy. *Healthy,* damn it. Without the colon issues that had plagued my parents. Meaning I might not die young, as they had. Maybe, just maybe, I'd broken the curse.

In the next few weeks, I began to feel something opening up within me. It was July, summer was in full swing, and it was almost as if I could feel my heart slowly unfurling. For the first time in a long time, I felt a sense of trust. I actually dared to hope I might live to an old age.

I began to sit outside more, letting the sun shine on my face. I could feel it, finally—life hovering within my grasp. One day, I even noticed I was laughing more. Something deep had shifted.

One afternoon in late summer, during one of the 15-minute crawl-into-bed breaks that I'd started referring to as bed therapy, I realized that I'd placed an incredible amount of pressure on my marriage by expecting Ken to give me unconditional love. I don't know how it was so clear to me suddenly, but for the first time, I *got* it, understood the root cause of my unreasonable expectations.

The truth was, *I* was the person who needed to give myself that kind of love and acceptance, not someone else. To do that, I had to treat myself with kindness and compassion. To accept my flaws alongside my gifts, loving them all the best I could.

Because when I rejected my flaws, I just rejected myself. And that was what I'd been doing for decades now. Keeping myself as stuck in my little box as my father had been in his.

No wonder my marriage had suffered—I'd expected Ken to fill the holes within me, when all along, that had been my job.

I sat up in bed. I was sure I wasn't the only one struggling with this dynamic, either. On some level, weren't we all searching for the unconditional love we'd felt as babies, when we were still considered whole and perfect and good, no matter what we said or did or wore or looked like? No matter who or *what* we were.

Until we could learn how to give ourselves that kind of love, we'd always be searching for someone else to do it. Someone else to see the light inside us, someone else to remind of us of our beauty and our preciousness. Someone else to remind us of our *worth*.

Before I knew it, summer had melted into fall. After a rocky transition back to school, the kids were settling into their new schedules, which included fall soccer practice. While Gabriel was in preschool four afternoons a week, I buckled down and wrote, carving out the psychological space that helped keep me grounded.

Before long, I began to notice that the mornings and evenings carried a new chill. Life was moving forward again. Meaning it was time to take stock of where I was and where I was going. Nine months had now passed since my mother's death. As much as I'd kicked and screamed, I'd also started to create a life without my mother. Even though my old identity had disintegrated, a new one hadn't yet crystallized in its place.

On certain days, this felt freeing beyond measure. On others, it was terrifying. After all, I had no idea how to get to where I was going. So I continued moving forward, step by step. Most days, I meditated, wrote and danced. I had completed the website for the "Remember" grief wristbands, and now I started to very simply promote them. I also started blogging about grief, and continued to chip away at the story that would one day become this book. And I worked on trusting that everything would work out.

Rituals. Symbols. I'd become obsessed with them as a way of containing and honoring my grief. Even though my black "Remember" bracelet had given me much solace over the past few months, I was starting to find that it no longer fulfilled the same need as it had in the beginning. I was changing, slowly coming back to life—a newer, much richer life—and I wasn't sure I needed such a stark physical reminder of my grief.

One afternoon, at a local fair-trade shop, I found myself drawn to a simple woven leather bracelet comprised of white seed beads. I slipped it on my wrist, next to my black "Remember" bracelet. Perfect. Now I was wearing both sides of the story: life as well as death. In this way, I could honor the part of me that was still grieving while creating space for the part that was returning to life.

Will it come as any surprise that I started thinking about getting a tattoo next? The red streak in my hair had served its purpose, and I was ready to move on to something new. A tattoo felt like a fitting replacement.

But what? I'd never gotten a tattoo before because I'd never been able to decide on an image. Even though I still had no idea what kind of tattoo I wanted, the feeling only intensified. I was now 43 years old. If I didn't get a tattoo now, then when?

After weeks of looking at various images, asking for tattoo artist recommendations and visiting tattoo shops, I decided to order a batch of temporary tattoos so that I could test out a host of different symbols and designs.

When the tattoos arrived, we had a lot of fun placing them on our bodies. Nico and Gabriel were masters at putting on temporary tattoos with wet washcloths, and before long, their arms were covered with all sorts of skulls and animals.

As the kids were covering themselves with images, Ken helped me put an Ed Hardy, Americana-style "MOM" temporary tattoo on the back of my left shoulder. The word "MOM" was etched into a heart surrounded by flowers, and as soon as I saw it, it made me immensely happy. The tattoo was all of my favorite colors—orange, red, green and yellow—and three inches by three inches in diameter, a fuck-you to the good-girl I'd tried so hard to be. I loved it.

Each tattoo lasted about a week, and for weeks, I wore alternating tattoos in different places—a red henna tattoo circling my bicep, one over my heart, a vine tattoo on my back.

Most of the tattoos were hidden under my regular clothes, and I inadvertently debuted the rest in my dance class, where I received all sorts of compliments. People wanted to know if they were new, or if they simply hadn't noticed. After I sheepishly explained that they were temporary tattoos I was test-driving, we all had a good laugh.

People loved the idea of test-driving a tattoo before going for the real thing, so I brought in the extras. A kind man in his 60s chose a skull tattoo to freak out his adult children the next time they visited, while another dancer wanted a tattoo because she was coming out of a nasty divorce.

Over the next few weeks, I continued to try out different tattoos, but none of them moved me like the first "MOM" tattoo I'd placed on my shoulder. So I made an appointment with a well-respected tattoo artist in town. The wait list to get in to see him was six months. I could get in with someone else much sooner, but I wanted to make sure I wasn't making a mistake.

For months, I'd been stocking up on books about forgiveness, trying to force a new level of healing with my parents. I was tired of digging through the past, trying to come to terms with all the issues I hadn't been able to resolve when my parents were still alive, and I just wanted to be *done with it* already. But I could never stick with any of the books, and it wasn't long before I'd discard one book in search of the next.

Despite that, I found myself thinking about the topic of forgiveness on an almost daily basis. One afternoon, in a fit of optimism, I texted Arielle that I was ready to forgive my parents. "How do I do that?" I typed. As if it were a question she could answer in a sentence or two.

By the time my next appointment rolled around, I was berating myself for thinking I could simply snap my fingers and be done with it.

Arielle was much more compassionate. "You keep doing exactly what you're doing," she told me. "Recognizing the patterns, uncovering the pain and releasing it. Bit by bit, you'll get there."

One afternoon, after picking up the kids from school, feeding them a snack and settling them in front of a short video, I was lying in bed taking one of my 15-minute bed-therapy breaks when I felt the connection between me and my mother break. It was the strangest sensation, as if an energetic cord had snapped and separated just above my belly button. My umbilical cord. My last energetic connection to my mother, finally severed.

My mind felt clear and strong. There was no mistaking what had just happened. Why now, I wondered. Was it because I was feeling stronger? Or because I'd finally become independent from my mother in a way I'd never managed while she was alive?

I rose and went to the window. The sky was streaked with pink. Alpenglow.

CHAPTER 11

FLOOD

In the middle of the night, a beeping water sensor from the basement awoke me. I stumbled downstairs to see water pouring in from one of the casement windows in our basement. The carpet was darkened and bruised, covered in two inches of water.

It was 1:00 a.m. Outside, the rain continued to pound down after two straight days of pouring rain. I stared at the scene for a moment in shock, not quite understanding what I was seeing. A small river, coming through the cracks of our window.

I ran to wake up Ken, who grabbed a giant bucket before heading into the driving rain. While he went to pinpoint the source of the water, I scoured the house for flashlights. The kids had taken them all for their forts, and in my panic, all I could find was a flickering blue plastic flashlight that barely worked.

I headed outside and joined Ken by the window well, now three feet deep in water. As he climbed down into the well, our neighbor's voice rang out in the darkness, asking if we needed help. Yes, I said, we need flashlights!

Kate was over in minutes. Her husband John was helping another set of neighbors whose basement window had blown open from the water pressure, filling their basement with four feet of glass, mud and water, Kate said as she handed me an industrial flashlight. Ken reached up, handing me a full bucket of water, and for the next hour, we worked as a team, bailing out the window well. Kate had brought over additional buckets along with the flashlights, and she and John raced back and forth between our houses.

The 2013 Colorado Floods, as this act of nature would soon become known, had arrived on the heels of a drought, a year after a catastrophic fire had wiped out the mountainside surrounding Boulder. Without the trees and foliage that normally absorbed excess water, conditions had been ripe on all levels for a flash flood.

Of course, Ken and I knew none of this as we raced to stop the flooding. By morning, we'd realized how lucky we were to have gotten off with such minor damage while people were being evacuated and losing their homes. The rain continued for another 24 hours as we anxiously monitored the news. There was no break, just more flooding and pounding rain amidst washed out streets and intersections.

Occasional sirens warned of new flash floods. Evacuations continued across the foothills and lost homes increased by the hour. Fatalities began to appear on the news. Many of the foothill roads above our town had washed out or collapsed. At one point, there was a 20-foot wall of water coming down Boulder Canyon.

By the time the rains finally eased 24 hours later, eight people had been killed. Two thousand homes had been lost, with thousands of people evacuated or displaced. The damage was estimated to be over $2 billion, with 200 miles of roads washed out and approximately 19,000 homes damaged. The National Guard spent a full week flying rescue missions into the mountains, in the largest national air lift since Hurricane Katrina, rescuing 3000 people and 900 pets as we listened to the sound of Chinooks and Blackhawks buzzing overhead.

Once the rains finally subsided, we ventured outside to survey the damage. The aftermath was incredible, apocalyptic in some areas, with varying levels of destruction everywhere I turned. Nico's elementary school, three blocks from our home, had swelled into a lake, with three feet of standing water in many of the classrooms. The school would remain closed for nearly three weeks; flood mitigation firms would remain on the premises, working around the clock in multiple shifts, 24-hours a day, seven days a week, for months.

Major thoroughfares were strewn with mud and debris; standing water receded slowly. The mood on the streets was somber, revelatory. As often happens during crisis, people responded with incredible grace. We were now connected to strangers and neighbors in an entirely new way, and my heart brimmed with each new exchange, all of us reaching out to help each other in the aftermath. Volunteer Facebook groups devoted to digging out buried homes sprouted like mushrooms.

I kept this feeling, this thankfulness, close to my chest in the following weeks as we pulled up rancid carpet and tossed away wet and moldy belongings. Coming so soon after my mother's death, I found the flood especially poignant, yet another reminder that love and connection were what really mattered. Not things, but people.

Tanja Pajevic

Cleaning up from the flood wasn't easy work. The kids were home from school and regular life had ground to a halt. Friends and neighbors helped rip up carpet and shared tips on dealing with mold. In the midst of all this, I stumbled onto my mother's birthday. When I saw the date on the calendar, I couldn't believe I'd forgotten.

It was a surreal moment in a surreal week. I tried to be gentle with myself, remind myself that I'd given myself this entire first year to grieve, not just one day, but it wasn't long before I sunk into a funk. Everything I'd learned during the flood seemed to have evaporated, like the morning fog.

I needed some help finding my way forward, so before I went to bed that night, I prayed for guidance. Then I set my notebook and pen next to my pillow so I could capture any messages that appeared in my dreams.

When I awoke the next morning, I found a bunch of notes I'd scribbled in the middle of the night about how important it was that I keep writing. Above all, I'd been told, I needed to love myself.

I sighed. I was trying my best with that one, people. *Really.*

But at least I'd gotten some direction. Keep writing. Love yourself. The writing was easy—it kept me sane, especially since my mother had died. It was the loving myself that was hard. I stumbled downstairs, mulling over the night's dreams as I got the kids breakfast and started the day.

Mid-morning found us moving things out of my basement office so that we could rip out the last of the carpeting. The kids, home on an extended vacation because school was closed, were watching *Dinosaur Train.*

As Ken emptied my office bookshelves, I dove into the closet. It was filled with storage bins that had accumulated since having children, bins I'd meant to clear out once I had more time. I grabbed the first bin I saw—a jumble of work documents as well as medical forms from my pregnancy with Nico. A card was sitting atop the mess, positioned so that I couldn't miss it. I bent closer and picked it up. It was a Hallmark card my mother had given me in 1992, for my college graduation. What the hell was it doing here, mixed in with work and baby things?

"Dear Tanja," my mother had written atop the card:

> *I just wanted to tell you*
> *how proud I am of you.*
> *I know it's not easy for you,*
> *being pulled in so many*
> *different directions*
> *by so many responsibilities*
> *in your life.*
>
> *But you can do it …*
> *just keep holding tightly*
> *to your dream*
> *until it is no longer a dream,*
> *but a beautiful reality.*
>
> *There's a wonderful tomorrow*
> *just waiting for you.*
> *M.E. Miro*

The next day, I emailed Scott, a bereavement counselor I'd met in a class. Every so often, he reached out to see how I was doing. This was the first time I'd reached out to him, but I needed his help. That was one of the fundamental lessons the flood had taught me, that asking for help was critical to receiving.

I told Scott a bit about the flood, then shared how I'd been sidelined by my mother's birthday. What did he do for birthdays and anniversaries, I wanted to know. How did he *survive* them?

Scott told me how he celebrated his deceased mother's birthday by taking his family to her favorite Mexican restaurant. That way, she could still be with them. He'd also created photo books to share with his grandchildren, and he told lots of stories about his mother, to help them remember her as a real person.

I let this sink in.

What kinds of stories?

Stories about her personality, stories about her values and likes, lessons she'd taught him throughout his life. In this way, he could pass on the valuable information that tends to get lost throughout the generations.

For the next few weeks, I mulled this over. I already knew from my birthday freak-out that birthdays would be hard, and Scott's words gave me a new model for dealing with them. Rather than simply connecting to my mother in pain and sorrow—what I'd been doing so far—I could choose to connect to her through stories and laughter.

I kept Scott's words close to my chest in the coming weeks as we struggled to get a foothold on the basement. Like many other families affected by the flood, I'd filed FEMA paperwork requesting financial assistance. Because our losses had only been a few thousand dollars, I didn't know if we qualified, and was thankful to learn we'd been awarded a small amount of funding because both of our offices were located in the basement.

Despite that, most of my work had ground to a halt in the weeks the kids had been home. I'd set up a makeshift office on a folding table in our cramped bedroom, thinking I could work there while we recalibrated our basement, but I wasn't accomplishing much. Since I was self-employed, it was all too easy to put my work on the back burner, especially while the kids were home.

Ken, meanwhile, was still on the clock. He worked remotely for a global technology company, spending a good chunk of his day on conference calls in the basement. Now he was doing that work amidst piles of belongings, his desk atop a loud, barren, concrete floor as dehumidifiers droned in the background, and it was driving him nuts.

Ken has always been a night owl, and before long, he was spending his late-night hours researching what to do with the basement floor. After much back and forth, he'd decided to grind down the concrete and stain it instead of replacing the carpeting. That way, if it flooded again, we'd have a much easier cleanup.

Weeks passed while he continued his research, searching for the best method. I found it hard to imagine working in such chaotic surroundings, and was doing my best to support Ken even though I didn't quite get his obsession over the floor. To me, concrete was concrete; I was just thankful the damage hadn't been worse.

Despite the progress I was making in living my life more fully, the smallest things still possessed the ability to unhinge me. One early fall morning, I was sitting on the back deck meditating before Ken and the kids awoke. It was one of those quiet, overcast fall days when the trees were bare canopies of their previous selves. With no foliage to hide under, I felt exposed, too.

Even the light was different: thinner, more harsh. A single, dry leaf fell from the tree above me and hit the deck. The wind picked up, sending a battalion of leaves scampering after it. Something about the brittle, lonely sound symbolized everything that was wrong in my new life without my mother, and I burst into tears. Just like that, I was back in the hole. Again.

A few days later, I found out that Marko was also feeling the change of seasons, both of us thrown off balance by the transition. Forced to adjust to another cycle of life by ourselves, each new season a visceral reminder that my mother no longer lived among us.

Autumn had been my mother's favorite season, and one of my favorite times of year, too, with all my favorite colors. But now I found myself having flashbacks to the previous October, permanently etched into my head as The Dying Season. I couldn't look at a yellow tree without remembering the hellacious emergency surgery that had kicked off my mother's illness. Fall was now little more than a visceral reminder of the weeks and months we'd spent inside hospital rooms, watching the trees morph from spectacular canopies of color to empty spires.

Once again, I found myself burdened by the past, caught in memories from my mother's illness. The small moments of joy I'd so recently appreciated appeared fewer and further between.

One especially dark day, when none of my usual self-care tricks were working and I was sinking into the quicksand, I went up to my bedroom, shut the door and prayed.

When I was done, I grabbed a handful of snacks and piled the kids into the car so we could take Loki to the vet. The kids were quiet, chowing down their after-school snacks, and when I turned the radio on, the song "Hey Hey Hey" by Michael Franti & Spearhead was playing.

I cranked the volume. "Guys! It's Michael Franti!"

The kids knew how much I loved his music, and they sang along for a bit. His music had saved me after my mother's death, given me hope and possibility, and for a long time, I'd barely been able to listen to much else. Whenever I played one of his albums, Gabriel called it "mama's happy music."

Singing hey, hey, hey no matter how life is today
There's just one thing that I got to say
I won't let another moment slip away

Loki was sitting in the front seat next to me, smiling in the magical way that some dogs do. I reached over and stroked his golden fur, thankful for the song and the moment. Just then, a red-tailed hawk swooped down in front of the car and I swerved slightly, to avoid hitting the dead animal on the road ahead.

"Did you see that?" I screeched. The kids knew about the hawks, often pointing them out when I missed one. "That was crazy!"

After a quick peek, the kids retreated back into their own worlds, and I was still mulling over my near miss with the hawk as we pulled into the parking lot. As I was getting Loki out of the car, I looked up for a moment. An eagle, passing overhead.

My kids knew how much I missed my mom. I told them so often, without hesitation, partly because I wanted them to know that they weren't the source of my tears, but also because I knew I needed to show them a model for grieving. My research, as well as my work with Arielle, supported this. The only way to teach kids how to grieve was to model it—to show them that it was OK to cry. Now that I'd been in a somewhat more stable emotional space for the past few months, I'd found that the kids felt more room to express their own grief.

To further support them in their process, I'd created simple memory boxes for all three grandchildren, as Scott had suggested. To do this, I bought plastic bins from Target in the kids' favorite colors and filled them with baby photos of the kids with my mother. The boxes were theirs to do with as they pleased, whether that meant decorating them or filling them with letters or other mementos. The kids liked that, and every so often, I'd notice Nico or Gabriel looking at their photos.

The children's resilience continued to surprise me. Gabriel in particular was doing better every day. He'd finally settled into his last year of preschool and had become more comfortable with his school friends, as well as on the playdates that had taken a hit while my mother was dying.

Nico, always a sensitive soul, was doing well, too. Both kids had their moments when they lashed out or melted down, but overall, they were settling down from the trauma of the past year, solidifying into healthy, grounded children who continued to blow me away with their knowledge of what mattered and how the world worked.

One night, I was reading Nico a bedtime story when he said, "You know how we were talking about God a while back, Mom?"

I nodded.

"Well, here's how I think it works: God has a certain percentage of our souls." He looked up at me, all big brown eyes. "If God is inside us, then a part of us must be inside God."

Tears filled my eyes as I hugged him. It wasn't the first time Nico had blown me away with his old-soul wisdom, and it wouldn't be the last.

CHAPTER 12

A CLEAN SLATE

As often happens, nature shows us the way. After the hard work of pulling up our carpet and moving all of our basement belongings into the garage, I began to see the flood as a gift. A clean slate, a way to start over.

Time and space loomed before me. I still had another two months left before the first anniversary of my mother's death, and I wanted to make the most of it. Two months was both an eternity and nothing. How would I mark that time? And how would I know that I'd used that time to grieve well?

Meanwhile, Marko and I had finally found a beautiful hawk image for my mother's headstone. After multiple trips to the cemetery and a ridiculous amount of back and forth over fonts, spacing and filler artwork, we finally placed the order for my mother's headstone.

Now that we'd placed the headstone order with Olga, there was nothing else to do but wait. The war between Marko and Olga seemed to have reached a temporary ceasefire. The headstone would arrive by early December, in time for the first anniversary of my mother's death. Now we just had to decide how to mark it.

In the meantime, I'd found myself drawn to a meditation retreat taught by David Harshada Wagner, the meditation teacher I followed online. The retreat was at Kripalu, in the Berkshires of western Massachusetts, and it would be the first time I'd been on a plane away from my children. It wasn't an easy trip to pull off logistically, financially or emotionally, but the retreat felt increasingly important as the weeks leading up to my mother's anniversary slipped away, so we cashed in frequent flier miles and turned the trip into my Christmas present to make it happen.

The Big Heart Meditation Retreat, as Wagner called it, was meant to help us move past our fear so that we could live more fearlessly and powerfully. When I found out that David Kessler, one of my favorite grief writers, was holding a retreat at Kripalu that same weekend, I knew I was where I was supposed to be. Will it come as any surprise to learn that both retreats occurred on the Day of the Dead?

I settled into the retreat with a healthy amount of nervousness, wondering if I should have signed up for Kessler's workshop instead. Meanwhile, Wagner's workshop was starting to work its magic. There was a forgiveness meditation aimed at forgiving ourselves, as well as meditations around fear, gratitude and acceptance. We were even taught how to give ourselves loving, compassionate breath instead of beating ourselves up— something that had never come easily for me. As the hours wore on, something within me was starting to thaw.

Meanwhile, I was driving myself crazy debating whether or not I should jump ship and join the grief workshop instead. Finally, after I'd spent far too much time asking strangers what they thought I should do, I realized I needed to reclaim my power and decide for myself. My heart had been drawn to this Big Heart Retreat for one reason or another, and if I didn't commit to myself now, when would I?

Later that afternoon, I found my compromise when I chatted with David Kessler and his co-facilitator, John Holland, at a book signing. When I told David Kessler how much his book *Life Lessons* (co-written with Elisabeth Kübler-Ross) had helped me, he nodded in recognition.

"That's my favorite book," he said. "I wish I could live that way."

I looked at him, startled. "But you wrote it."

"Yeah, I know. But to live like that every day?" He shook his head. "On a good day, maybe. But it's like anything else."

He asked me if I had kids.

I nodded.

"It's like parenting. You know what you should do, but are you always able to do it? No. It's the same way."

It wasn't until the weekend was over that I understood the full extent of the gift he'd given me with his words. Kessler might have written that incredible book, yes, but he didn't hold himself to any unrealistic standards. He was a human being, after all; imperfect, just like the rest of us. And just like the rest of us, he was doing the best he could.

This was the same lesson I was learning in my meditation retreat. The sooner I could let myself off the hook for not being perfect, the sooner I'd be able to release others as well. Freedom would always come through compassion and self-acceptance, not fear and criticism.

As the retreat was winding down, Wagner explained that Buddhism and yoga come from a place of compassion—the belief that we're already perfect as we are right now, in this moment. In this belief system, our basic essence is goodness.

But most of us view life through another paradigm, one that teaches we're flawed. This paradigm believes that life is tough, and we must work hard because life *is* hard. The essence of this model isn't goodness and ease, as it is in Buddhism, but hard work punctuated by moments of enjoyment.

As we were preparing to head back into our real lives, Wagner asked us to consider integrating a different paradigm into our lives, the belief that life is an experience of joy, wonder, happiness and service punctuated by moments of forgetfulness.

I carried Wagner's message with me as we left Kripalu and boarded the airport shuttle. His words had moved me deeply, touched a part of myself that I hadn't been able to give voice to. Open, joyful, free, loving, realizing I was *good enough* as I was, flaws and all—this was how I wanted to live my life. I was done with the endless struggle, done with making things harder than they needed to be. I looked out the window, my head full of ideas. A road sign caught my attention. "New Plans. New Game."

Wagner had encouraged us to head home with a clear intention for the next few weeks, and I'd chosen to be kind to myself through Thanksgiving, something that felt manageable since it was only three weeks away.

Every morning, before the kids awoke, I started my day with a meditation. On the days I remembered the gratitude meditation Wagner had taught us as an antidote to fear, I found myself far more present and accepting. This helped the mood around our household immensely. The kids didn't act up nearly as much as they did when I was upset, and I was once again reminded what a petri dish we live in, all of us interconnected, our moods deeply affecting each other.

For those first few weeks, life was more calm and joyful than it had been in a long while. Life felt full again, open to possibility. I felt as if I could *do* this, actually be a motherless daughter. Become a fully-realized, fully-functioning person who happened to have lost both her parents.

And then the week of Thanksgiving hit, knocking me off feet. My first Thanksgiving without my mother—it was just too much. I wish I could say I remembered Wagner's teachings, but they all evaporated in the midst of my longing.

In the blink of an eye, I'd fallen back into the old ways that used to sustain me: anger, struggle, suffering. The mornings were so dark and cold that I began sleeping in and skipping my morning meditations. The more meditations I skipped, the easier it became to skip the rest of my self-care regime. My regular writing practice stopped and started multiple times. Life happened in painful fits and bursts. I was more melancholy, sad. Some days, I felt like I might explode. By the first week of December, I'd stopped writing entirely.

One afternoon, I passed my mother's condo after dropping Gabriel off at preschool, and started sobbing uncontrollably. Before long, my sobs turned into wails as I drove down the street, trying to get home. I couldn't remember ever having cried like this, not even as my mother was dying. Something had broken loose.

I didn't understand it until the following week, when an appointment with Arielle helped me realize the depth of that sorrow. Gabriel's fifth birthday was quickly approaching, raising another fresh wave of grief. My mother wouldn't be there for it. Never again would he have his beloved grandmother with him. This sucked to high heaven. Not only was this my loss, but my children's, too.

For days, I walked around with this thumping in my heart. I was angry, a pain in the ass to be around. Ken saw that I was going downhill, but he didn't have the energy to help. After much trial and error, he'd finally abandoned the idea of staining the concrete floor and had ordered carpeting for our basement, but the installation guy kept cancelling at the last minute. Working in our chaotic basement for the past two months had taken its toll on Ken, and he was starting to shut down alongside me.

As had happened during difficult times in the past, the general order of our house began to slide. With it went the rules. Instead of enforcing our usual screen time limits, we started letting the kids watch more and more videos. Meals became looser and looser until the kids were living on pizza and pasta. Winter break loomed on the horizon; with it, the first anniversary of my mother's death. It was so much. Too much.

I started escaping to my bedroom once, twice, three times a day. I spent more time wrapped in blankets, cancelled what few plans existed, and generally pulled back from that full life I'd been on the edge of living. My inner critic swelled up, loud and clear. I sucked. I was a terrible mother, a terrible person. Nobody else grieved like this. What was *wrong* with me?

Before long, I'd stopped writing altogether. My anger became deeper, more intense. I felt trapped, caught in a life with no escape. I yelled at the kids, apologized profusely, then did it again.

More anger, more grief, more inner critic. I was on an island, floating away, untethered, unreachable. I should run away, I thought. Get a divorce. On the worst of days, I thought perhaps I should kill myself. I knew that I wouldn't actually attempt suicide—knew that deeply after having been down this road with postpartum depression—but the appearance of those suicidal thoughts was a giant red flag, a sharp reminder it was time for an emergency appointment with Arielle.

As she'd done during my bout with postpartum depression, Arielle helped me see that my suicidal thoughts arose when I'd abandoned myself for days and weeks on end. I'd contacted her early enough this time around that she was able to help me pull out of my downward spiral quickly, and soon after that emergency session, I committed to writing and meditating regularly again.

Those writing sessions were magic. Each time I wrote tethered me to the ground. As the days wore on, I began to feel stronger, more able. I began to trust myself again. And I became more equipped to deal with the demands of the day, including my husband and children.

As it had done so many times before, writing gave me a container for my emotions. For a long time, I'd felt the need to write a scathing essay about the way our medical profession approaches death, and now I dove in with fury. I was still incensed about the way my mother's doctors had pretended they could corral death, keeping it at bay, when what we'd most needed at the time was someone to speak with us honestly as we tried to navigate death's waters.

As I got deeper and deeper into the medical essay, it became my lifeline back to the living. Now that I was grounded and functioning again, I could once again see some possibility. On a lark, I submitted a short essay and photo of my mother to "The Lives They Lived," a yearly tribute *The New York Times* ran to acknowledge recent losses.

And then my mother's headstone arrived. Whack, thump, and down I went; another move in this shitty dance that I couldn't quite seem to follow. Strong one day, collapsed the next.

Marko and I met at the cemetery to watch the cemetery workers place the headstone. It was a warm December day, another ordinary day for the workers who delivered the headstone with a small forklift and manually adjusted it into place. It was a physical job, and I watched in silence as they shifted and edged, lining the headstone up with the base. Finally, they applied some kind of caulk around the base to keep it sealed and connected. They were nice guys, chatting with Marko about all the ways Boulder had changed over the years, but I couldn't join their conversation. It felt too surreal.

The headstone was a beautiful gray stone flecked with white. Etched flowers surrounded my mother's name, and a strong, fierce hawk was etched onto the back. It was exactly what we'd wanted, and I felt a strong shiver pass through my body as I gazed at the headstone.

How was this possible? How was it possible that my mother was truly dead, buried beneath this terrible patch of earth?

A week later, Marko and I met at the gravesite with our families to mark the first anniversary of my mother's death. We'd asked Father Seraphim, the upbeat, laughing priest we'd met the previous year, to perform a short graveside service. Neither one of us had the energy for a Serbian *parastos*, a traditional memorial service held at church, which includes homemade bread and *žito*, a sweetened, boiled wheat dish ground with walnuts. As we'd done with my mother's funeral, we'd decided to celebrate her outside in nature, but this time with a kind, compassionate priest.

The day was bitterly windy and cold, all the more so at the cemetery. Our thick winter coats barely deflected the harsh wind, and Father Seraphim couldn't keep his candle lit, although we were all gathered around him, trying to help. As such, the ceremony was even shorter than the 20-minute ceremony we'd planned, and I couldn't help but compare it to my mother's burial.

When the service was over, we stood next to our cars, shivering, trying to figure out what to do next. Father Seraphim had moved on to his next obligation, so Marko and I took our families to a local brewpub for burgers and beer, something we both felt my mother would have appreciated. But that, too, didn't feel quite right.

On the way home, I felt grumpy, unsettled. What had we been trying to do, anyway, I wondered, celebrate my mother's life or celebrate her death? It all felt so strange and anticlimactic. Empty. I wanted to do more. But I didn't know what.

So I shared this with Arielle during our next session. As always, she extended more compassion than I was capable of giving myself, suggesting that perhaps going easy on myself might be a way of honoring my mother. For days afterward, I mulled this over. I liked the idea of being kinder and gentler with myself. I wanted to believe it was possible.

But this had been the first anniversary of my mother's death—a big, important marker. And I had to be the good daughter. Meaning I had to honor her in just the right way. But *how*? What?

The days wore on. Christmas, just a week away, no longer felt important, not with its bitter representation of my mother's death. December was a time of mourning for me now, not celebration.

But the kids weren't having any of my attempts to ignore the holidays. At ages five and seven, they were squarely into Santa and gifts and Christmas trees and wrapping. So Ken and I rallied and bought a tree, put lights on it and called it a day. The kids were the ones who insisted we add ornaments.

With their insistent pressure, we began to feel a bit of the holiday cheer. Whether or not I'd done it right, we'd passed the first anniversary of my mother's death. I began to feel a bit more space, as if I no longer had to hold my breath.

One night, Ken stumbled onto *A Charlie Brown Christmas*, one of my mother's favorite holiday shows. My mother had always wanted us to watch it with the kids, but for various reasons, we never had. Nico in particular had been dead set against it.

Not this year. For the first time, he was entranced by the show. We all were. I sat between Nico and Gabriel on our brown, beaten down couch, amidst the ghosts of my childhood, crying for Charlie Brown, but also for my mother, her spirit thick between us.

Afterward, Ken and I admitted we'd both felt my mother's presence. The show had felt like a gift from her, dropped into our laps out of the blue. We so rarely watched regular TV that I don't know how Ken stumbled upon it.

The next morning, I received an email from an editor at the online site *Gawker* accepting one of my essays for publication. The essay, "What My Mother's Death Taught Me About Life," was a personal account of how I'd decided to free myself from the family patterns that had enchained my parents. It delved into my family's lifelong penchant for suffering and explored our history, Serbian ethnicity, our relationship with money, and all sorts of other self-sabotaging behaviors I'd adopted in a misguided attempt at staying connected with my family. In short, it was a manifesto about breaking free from the past and finally living my own life. I'd submitted the essay the previous February, and had assumed they didn't want it.

They did—as long as I could substantially edit it down so that they could run it the following day. So I set the kids up with some videos and dove in. By dinnertime, I still had a final round of edits to go. On a whim, Ken looked up the night's programming and found that *It's a Wonderful Life*, my mother's favorite movie, was on TV.

"I'll put the kids to bed," he said. "You go watch it."

"But I have to finish revising this essay."

Ken shook his head. "You have to watch it," he said. "What are the chances that I just happened to look it up—"

"And that it's on tonight?"

"Yeah."

I sighed.

"You've gotta watch it," he repeated. "For your mom."

"You're right," I said. "I'll finish my final edits during commercials."

In the movie, an angel named Clarence helps kind, compassionate and increasingly frustrated businessman George Bailey see what life would have been like if he'd never existed. For a good chunk of my life, my mother and I had watched this post-WW-II exploration of close relationships together, and this year, I settled in alone, tears in my eyes as I watched George Bailey consider suicide after his financial life fell apart.

Watching another person battle suicidal thoughts after I'd so recently faced them myself was sobering, and I couldn't help but feel like my mother was speaking to me through the movie, showing me what a mistake it was to have even considered taking my own life. Perhaps, like George, I, too, had my own guardian angel. Perhaps, like George, I was too buried in my own misery to see the joy and love that surrounded me.

Tears streamed down my face as I watched Clarence work to open George's heart, to show him that whatever dark night he was facing, it would always turn out all right.

As the credits rolled across the screen, I finished my final edits and emailed off my essay. It ran the next day, on Winter Solstice, exactly one year after we'd buried my mother. Seventy thousand people read it, and for days afterward I received moving messages from readers about how much my essay had helped them. Not for one second did I think my mother wasn't behind its success.

CHAPTER 13

BEGINNINGS AND ENDINGS

A few days before the New Year, we flew to the Midwest to visit friends. The trip was a hot mess from the start, with our kids waking at 5:00 a.m. while our night-owl hosts slept in till 9:00 a.m. If you've ever traveled with young children, you know what a nightmare it can be trying to keep them quiet in someone else's home. We did what we could by putting them in front of videos for hours instead of our usual 30-minute limit, but by the time our hosts arose, our kids were freaking out from the overdose of screen time and were melting down like crazy. The worse their temper tantrums became, the more uptight and critical I became, until we were caught in our old vicious cycle.

I was still feeling vulnerable from the first anniversary of my mother's death, and it was only making things worse. On the rare occasion I mentioned my mother, the conversation quickly dead-ended, and I soon realized that our friends weren't comfortable with grief.

Then I received an email confirming that the photo and short piece I'd submitted to *The New York Times* honoring my mother's life had been accepted. I was standing in the kitchen, checking email on my phone when I saw the message, and I showed it to Ken, bubbling with excitement. Finally, I'd done something worthwhile to honor my mother's life. For a brief moment, I felt so proud.

Just then, our friend walked into the kitchen. I told her my news, showing her the published photo of my mother.

"Oh," she said, leaning over to take a quick peek. "That's nice." And then she once again changed the topic.

My heart dropped, and I was overcome with a deep wave of shame. This was the *third* time I'd mentioned my mother during this visit—three fucking times—and damned if I was going to make that mistake again. I walked out of the kitchen in a quiet cloud of anger. If my heart wasn't welcome here, I decided, neither was I.

Over the next few days, I began to shut down, contort myself into the helpful, invisible houseguest I assumed our friends wanted. To do this, I no longer took care of myself in my grief, checking out emotionally instead. At night, I drank too much wine; in the mornings, too much coffee. I went through the days in my parallel world, distant and alone. By the fourth day of our seven-day trip, Ken and I were arguing bitterly and I was fantasizing about flying home early with the kids.

That night, a deep, God-like voice awoke me from my dreams. *"Do not abandon oneself."* I sat up in shock, the deep, regal bass unlike anything I'd ever heard. For a few minutes, I simply drank it in, awestruck by the perfectness of that message.

This whole trip, I'd been blaming everyone else for my unhappiness. But *I* was the one who'd abdicated responsibility by not taking care of myself. If I'd just taken the time to write, meditate or exercise, a lot of my suffering could have been avoided.

Yes, my hosts hadn't supported me in my grief. But much worse, I hadn't supported myself. By trying to act like someone I wasn't, I'd abandoned myself. And someone—God?—had called me on it.

After we returned from the Midwest, I turned all my yucky energy toward getting us back on track. Ken and I resurrected the TV and video limits we'd ignored over the holidays, and the kids start settling down almost immediately. I also started cooking again—not the crazy, involved Serbian meals I'd been obsessed with the previous year, just basic meals like chicken, rice, salad and the occasional vegetable, anything to get the kids away from their holiday diet of pizza, pasta and sugar. And for the first time in two weeks, I went back to my dance class.

I eased into a hamstring stretch as I looked around the dance room. Regulars were trading greetings and asking about the holidays. One woman was sharing a harrowing story about her impending divorce while another was counting down the days until school started again. The holidays had been rough on plenty of others; I wasn't the only one who looked a little rough around the edges.

An hour later, sated and sweaty after we'd cooled down, I took stock. I was back in my body again, thank God, grounded after these last few painful, shiftless weeks. My mind felt clear and clean.

Once again, I looked around the room. Friends were chatting and smiling as they said their goodbyes. Relief was palpable on multiple faces. One woman had tears in her eyes as she pulled on her boots. Oh, boy, had I been there. You never knew which song or movement would trigger what; it was all part of the alchemy. Even though the feelings could be challenging, I always felt better after moving through them.

Once school started back up after the break, the carpet guys finally showed up to install our new basement carpet. As soon as they were done, we moved Ken's office furniture back into its designated space, and almost instantaneously, Ken began to relax.

Now that Ken wasn't so stressed, I felt lighter, too, and it became easier to focus on taking care of myself again. To get started, I pulled out my notes from my meditation retreat, and was shocked to realize how far I'd fallen off track. Instead of being kind and compassionate with myself, I'd become highly self-critical, especially during our trip to the Midwest, and instead of operating with an open heart, I'd closed down into a bitter bundle of fear.

It was a sobering moment. I had a choice, clearly. And fear and criticism weren't what I wanted for my life.

So I started again by recommitting to myself. I would wake up 15 minutes earlier in the morning so that I could meditate before my children awoke. And I left my Kripalu notes where I could see them the next time the going got rough. This time around, I wanted to remember to be kind to myself. To remember the Buddhist belief that at our very essence, we are all good. I wanted to remember that life really *could* be joyful, that it wasn't just about suffering and more suffering.

After meditating one morning, I remembered an exchange between my mother and Jeremy after his brother had died. Jeremy had been having a hard time making sense of his brother's death, and as he'd done so many times over the years, he'd come to my mother for help.

"You can't give up," my mother told him. "Your brother wouldn't have wanted you to throw away your life. The way you honor him is by living your life, Jeremy. Really, *fully* living your life."

He looked at her through tears. "But it's not fair that I'm still alive and he isn't."

"That's why it's so important that you live." She was intense with him, adamant. "He no longer has that choice. *But you do.*"

He shook his head.

"Don't let his death have been in vain," she insisted. "Honor his memory by living your life. By doing the best that you can."

I stood up from the couch. My mother's words weren't only for Jeremy. They were for me, too.

Meanwhile, we were still facing down the Serbian holidays: Christmas on January 7th, New Year's on January 14th and *Slava*, a holiday celebrating our family's patron saint, St. John the Baptist, on January 20th.

Neither Marko nor I wanted to celebrate the Serbian holidays with a small family dinner, as we'd done in the past. It just felt too painful without my mother. But we didn't want to ignore the holidays, either. After some discussion, we decided to roll the three holidays into one, throwing a combined Serbian Christmas, New Year's and *Slava* party.

Because the *Slava* was the biggest celebration of the three, we let that guide our preparations. For Serbs, the *Slava* is an important church holiday that's celebrated with a short church service, a giant party, tons of food and a houseful of family and friends. When we were kids, my parents had pulled out all the stops, and Marko and I wanted to do the same, albeit it with our own modifications. Instead of a week's worth of cooking, for example, we pared down our menu to only the most important dishes. And we threw the patriarchal gender roles of the day out the window, with Marko preparing the two most important dishes, the sweetened, ground wheat *žito* and the *Slavski kolač*, or *Slava* bread.

Thank God for Google. My mother had always cooked from memory, so Marko cobbled his version of the *Slava* bread together from some recipes he found online. My mother's *Slava* bread was one more recipe lost in the ether, as was the intricate design she'd used to decorate the bread, so Marko created his own. He did the same with the *žito*, a dish that was supposed to represent life, death and the resurrection of Christ.

Neither one of us had given much thought to the religious roots of the day until we started our online search. As Marko was digging around for recipes, I learned that the *Slava* celebration represents the day each family was baptized into Christianity. Traditionally, it's a day that connects us to our ancestors. Furthermore, the only other time it's appropriate to serve *žito* is for *parastos*, a memorial service honoring the dead. Once I read that, I wondered what we'd gotten ourselves into. Who exactly was driving this *Slava*? Us, or our ancestors?

Ken and I spent the week before the party reassembling our basement. We'd painted the walls sage green, and now we moved my mother's burgundy couches back in, then set up our bookshelves and rehung our paintings. It was an intensive task, and I quickly felt the weight of it. Ken and I were literally creating a new foundation beneath us, and it felt great. Instead of the cluttered, messy basement we'd had before, our basement was now a calm, organized space.

Our new basement inspired me so much that I decided to declutter the first floor as well. It had been years since we'd cleared out the kids' old toys, and I did so now with a vengeance, placing bag after bag aside for donation. Yes, the flood had been a major pain in the ass, but it had also forced us to get rid of all sorts of junk, and for that, I was grateful. To start over again felt like a giant gift.

The afternoon before the party, we started cooking. We'd decided (no surprise) to skip the church ceremony, focusing on the food instead. While Marko prepared the *žito* and baked the *Slava* bread, I taught Leslie how to make cheese *pita*, a savory dessert of phyllo dough and various cheeses, and one of my all-time favorites dishes. We made pan after pan of *pita*, carefully wrapping layers of phyllo around a mixture of butter, egg, feta, cottage and mozzarella cheeses. It was a labor-intensive process to keep each sheet of phyllo from drying out and breaking, and Ken put the kids to sleep as Leslie and I worked into the night, just like my mother had in the years before.

The morning of the party, I could feel my mother's spirit around me as I rushed around in preparation, as countless generations of women had done before me, cleaning, as my mother used to say, like a crazy Serbian woman. I even found myself talking like my mother, bossing people around as she'd done before a big party. I joked that I was channeling my mom, but it wasn't much of a joke. I was even on the verge of a migraine, as my mother had been before every big party she'd ever hosted.

So, as she'd done years before, I brewed myself a super-strong cup of coffee and drank it down with some aspirin, hoping that would kill my headache. Then I did my best to breathe once friends and neighbors started arriving.

As soon as new guests arrived, I brought them into the dining room, explained that John the Baptist was our patron saint, and offered them the traditional spoonful of *žito*. Then, like every good Serb before me, I offered them a shot of *Šlivovitz*. The Serbs are nothing if not drinkers, and it's not a party if it doesn't involve Serbian plum brandy.

As guests milled about snacking on appetizers—including *ajvar*, a Balkan delicacy made from roasted red peppers and garlic that I'd found at a specialty store—Ken grilled salmon for the adults and hot dogs for the kids. We filled in the rest with basics like rice and salad. Our lowered standards meant that the *Slava* bread, *žito* and *pita* were the stars of this party; everything else, we figured, could be solved with soda for the kids and wine or beer for the adults.

That was how the old-school *Slavas* had unfolded when we were children, adults milling about the main floor while children raced up and down the stairs, wild and unsupervised, and it made me happy to see it happening again in my home. Our house was packed with friends and neighbors, and I felt happy that so many folks had come out to celebrate with us. Even though we hadn't intended to create an authentic *Slava*, that's what ended up happening.

Was it just the sheer act of pulling together the pieces? The symbolism behind the entire day? The fact that Marko and I finally stepped forward to host *Slava* on our own terms?

Whatever it was, the night was a turning point for me. Instead of joking about my heritage (as I'd done so many times in the past), or sharing bits and pieces with carefully-culled friends, I'd opened my heart to all of it, celebrating our Serbian heritage in a way that not only honored me and my current family, but also my first family. It felt like the start of a wonderful new tradition.

Now that our *Slava* was behind us, I was hit by a wave of memories I didn't seem able to control. The memory of my mother's final week of life, brutally shortened by the last-ditch chemo effort the doctors had given her in an attempt to extend her life. Why hadn't those doctors sat us down and told us what would happen if that "effort" didn't work?

We'd been gambling, playing Russian roulette with my mother's life, hoping the chemo would buy her a little more time. Instead, she never came out of that chemo-induced hell, spending her final week going in and out of consciousness.

I lay in bed for nights, torturing myself over that simple, stupid decision, consumed by visions of my emaciated mother in those final days, how terribly she'd suffered from the chemo, rocked by anger toward her doctors, an even deeper anger toward myself, that I'd allowed that to happen. Wouldn't a natural death have been better?

I was awash in pain until a voice inside my head finally stopped me. "That was a gift," it said, "so she didn't have to suffer any more."

A gift, I thought. What kind of gift?

After a while, I remembered a story I'd heard about Elisabeth Kübler-Ross.

For years, she'd been angry with God for having made her mother suffer toward the end of her life. Then, during her own near-death experience, God told Kübler-Ross that her mother's suffering had been a gift, meant to teach her how to accept love in this lifetime, so she wouldn't have to learn it in the next.

Remembering this broke my heart wide open. Learning to receive love and support had been one of my mother's greatest challenges. What if that god-awful, horrible last week truly *had* been a gift?

I let this possibility float around in my mind for the next few days, rising to the surface when I was ready to re-inspect it, letting it settle when I wasn't. This new narrative felt better than the alternative, that was for sure.

And yet, I didn't realize how fully it had taken hold until the following week, when I took Gabriel in for his annual well visit.

Janet, the pediatric nurse, commented on how healthy Gabriel was. "Remember how often you were here last year?"

Did I.

"I know you were going through a lot with having just lost your mother," she said.

I nodded, partly because I didn't know what to say and partly because I didn't trust what I would say. Coming back to this combined hospital/medical facility so many times right after my mother died had stretched me to my limit.

"It's great to see that you're doing so much better."

"Thanks," I said. "I appreciate that." And I did. Her words were a stark reminder of how far we'd come.

On our way out of the pediatrician's office, I looked down the hallway to the cancer ward. How much that hallway had haunted me last year. I'd seen my mother everywhere I turned, the specter of her in every window, every patient I laid eyes on.

I looked down the hall once again.

Nothing. She was gone now. The hallway felt like a regular hallway again: calm, neutral, normal. I took this as a sign of healing, and sent up a silent *thank you* as Gabriel pulled me out the door.

Bit by bit, I began to notice that the grief seemed to run at a lower level, almost like a background program on a computer, one punctuated by periods of joy. Overall, I felt much calmer and more present, and I was beginning to see a shift in my relationship with the kids as well. Instead of harping on them, as I'd been doing for weeks, I was consciously focusing on being more positive. I still made plenty of mistakes, but I was starting to see that every time I was mad at myself, I took it out on Ken or the kids. My work with Arielle was helping me see that the self-criticism and anger I felt toward myself tended to appear when I tried to bypass my feelings.

So I kept working on it, letting myself feel the anger, the rage, the helplessness. Opening my heart to the possibility that it was safe to feel my feelings, that I alone knew how to take care of myself—with kindness and compassion, no less. That I alone knew what was best for me.

Bit by bit, day by day. Placing my hand over my heart when I felt another wave coming, taking a moment to go outside and breathe some fresh air or feel the sun on my face when I felt so trapped I feared I might go crazy. Saying no to a commitment I didn't want to make in the first place. Dancing, writing, meditating, each day waking up and trying again. Step by step, day by day.

Then, wham—another brutal memory. My mother, fighting the intense nausea that characterized the last three months of her life. It was one of the hardest parts of her illness, when neither the Zofran nor other anti-nausea medicines had helped.

Watching my mother struggle with that level of constant nausea about did me in. There was nothing I could do except sit with her, a container to her mouth as she spit up, my hand on her back as the waves of nausea crescendoed, feeling helpless as hell.

And just to make sure I understood exactly what she was going through, the universe had put me through my own paces the year before, when the kids and I got hit with *six* rounds of gastrointestinal bugs in the span of a few short months. Midway through that nasty autumn, I'd gotten food poisoning at a local restaurant. After six rounds of GI distress, I was beyond distraught when I felt the seventh coming.

As I entered that initial stage of shakiness and nausea that characterizes the arrival of a gastrointestinal bug, my heart plummeted. I couldn't do this again, I just couldn't. Seven times in two months was simply too much. I didn't know what I was supposed to be learning, but I got it.

Please God, I prayed, *I get it. I get whatever it is you're trying to teach me here. I've learned my lesson. Please make it go away. Please make it end.*

I crawled back into bed after vomiting and sent up one last prayer. Please God, I get it. I *get* it.

Then I fell into a hazy sleep, waiting for the next wave of nausea to strike. At some point, I half-awoke to feel my entire body ablaze with energy. My body was alive with an intense tingling that I'd never before felt, and my limbs felt awake with it, revitalized. I was awake enough to know that I wasn't dreaming, but I wasn't afraid. It felt like someone or something was helping me, sending this magnificent force throughout my body.

The next time I awoke, it was morning. By some miracle, I'd slept through the night. That had never happened before—it usually took me a good four to six hours to get past those initial, awful stages of a GI bug and get some sleep.

And then I remembered the magical tingling feeling from the middle of the night.

I'd been healed. I don't know how else to say it. Someone or something had answered my prayers, healing my body.

I often thought of this experience as my mother was dying. That stretch of illness had instilled a deep compassion within me that would become critical while my mother was dying. Day after day, week after week, I sat with my mother as she fought the waves of nausea, wiping her mouth after she'd vomited, rubbing her back. And I didn't walk away when others did. I understood her struggle all too well.

Shortly after Gabriel's five-year well visit, I was back at the same medical complex for my annual OB/GYN visit. The doctor's office was across the courtyard from the hospital, and as I walked out of my doctor's third-floor office, I was stunned to find myself standing directly across the courtyard from the maternity ward where my children had been born. Across that tiny little field were the exact rooms where I'd spent the first few days of their lives. There, at the curve of the building, was the maternity lounge where I'd snuck a snack while laboring with Nico.

One floor below that maternity ward stood the cancer ward. And there, in the exact same crook of the building, was another, more sober lounge, the place where Marko and I had held numerous meetings with a social worker about my mother's dwindling options.

Looking at those competing memories, juxtaposed in such a brilliant and brutal way, nearly took my breath away. I felt as if I was looking directly into my past, simultaneously viewing the most wonderful and awful days of my life at once.

Waves of joy and gratitude washed over me as I remembered holding Nico for the very first time. Then there was the fear and worry from Gabriel's high-risk pregnancy and our three hospital stays from complications with placenta previa and preterm labor, followed by deep relief after he pulled through an emergency cesarean section a month early. And there, in that corner—oh!—was all the intense love and sorrow of telling my mother how much I loved and appreciated her, all of my preparations for our long goodbye.

There was so much love looking back at me that I felt as if my heart would burst. Perhaps this is what it was like to die, I thought. Beginnings and endings, stretching as far as the eye could see.

CHAPTER 14

THE WAY FORWARD

Shortly after my profound hospital experience, the "Remember" wristband I'd been wearing for the past few months disappeared during my dance class. I looked around in surprise, thinking it must have flown off when I'd stretched my arms overhead, but there was nothing on the floor around me. The woman behind me saw me and joined in the search.

She hadn't seen it, either. No one had. By the time my dance class had wrapped up, its disappearance felt right. Even though I'd been thinking about taking off that wristband ever since the Serbian holidays, I hadn't been able to do it. This was the nudge I'd needed.

February. As the 21st anniversary of my father's death approached, I debated how to mark it. I'd been thinking a lot about ceremony and ritual and wanted to do something special, but wasn't sure what. As I was mulling this over, I realized how little my children knew about my father. I hardly ever spoke about him, and we didn't even have a photo of him up in our house.

175

So I started by filling in the gaps, telling my kids that even though we hadn't had a good relationship, my father had been quite a character. I told them about his teen years playing semi-professional soccer in the former Yugoslavia, then explained that he'd lived in Paris for three years before moving to the U.S. and opening a photography studio in Chicago. A few years after Marko's birth, he transitioned back into mechanical engineering, the work he'd originally been trained to do. Surely, Gabriel had inherited some of his physical acumen. And Nico? Just like my father, he was a master builder. Ever since Nico was a toddler, he could fashion anything with his hands.

The kids loved hearing about him, so I shared the rest of the stories I remembered. I told them about the designs and patents he'd created before his machining business went bankrupt, and we all laughed over the dog-pooper scooper he'd created. Less amusing was the "jumping shoe" my father had worked on for years, a gym shoe with springs in the sole to improve performance. The shoe had been his muse during the late 70s and early 80s, and it was a prototype of the Air Jordan before Air Jordans appeared on the market. For a long time, it haunted me that my father never profited from it.

Shortly after Ken and I became engaged, Ken looked up the patent, and found that my father's jumping shoe was nearly identical to the Air Jordan. If we'd found that patent earlier, Marko and I might have been able to sue Nike for a fraction of its earnings. By the time Ken found it, the patent had long expired, as had my father, who'd died nearly broke and on Medicaid.

For so long, my narrative about my father had portrayed him as a genius who hadn't been able to live among men. My sympathy for him went deep, and I did my best to share this with my children as I told them about my grandmother, who'd been killed in WWII when my father was young.

As I introduced my children to my father's ghost, I pulled out the old photos from the back of my closet, where they'd lived since the basement flood, and began to sift through them with anticipation. But instead of finding the man I'd romanticized in my tales, I found a man driven by his ego. There were black and whites of my father in Paris, arty self-portraits in his Chicago photography studio, *Paul's Studio de Paris*, and self-portraits at the drafting board in his tool and die, *Proto Precision*. When he wasn't alone, he was surrounded by employees or girlfriends.

Who had taken these photos? And how had I forgotten about this side of my father, the ceaseless, egomaniac who could never get enough, make enough, *be* enough.

It wasn't as if he didn't try. Things are lookin' up, he'd said to me on a near-daily basis. One day soon—I promise—we'll have a nicer house. And a pool! Soon, *zlato*, you'll see.

As a child, I could've cared less about a new house or a pool—all I wanted was for my father to spend time with me. But he was always at work, chasing some new dream.

My anger was growing. I lifted another handful of photos and sifted through them. More women from his life after us. There he is, my father, fully gray in his early 50s, three or four girlfriends I hadn't known about in the short span between my mother and my stepmother.

Another woman, another glass of wine. That smile, once so charming, now thin, forced. He still had those same, smiling eyes, but they were flatter, and even I could tell he was trying too hard. Disappearing before the camera, trying to pretend he mattered. It sickened me.

What? I sat up. Where did *that* come from?

"Sickening" had been one of my father's favorite phrases, a term I never, ever used. My father had been a highly critical man, constantly on us for one thing or another, and I could still feel the burn of it.

For so long, I'd excused that side of him, told myself that those critical ways were a terrible byproduct of having lost his mother at such a young age. And while that may have been true, I was pissed about what that heavy criticism had cost me.

Yes, my father had been wounded. We all had. But he'd never stepped up, dealt with his shit so that the rest of my family wouldn't have to. And here I was, 21 years later, still paying the price.

What a load of bullshit.

Infuriated, I threw the photos back into the box and shoved them into the back of my closet. What an asshole. I couldn't believe how angry I was, what a deep well of anger I'd uncovered.

As I was grappling with that anger, a friend turned me on to *The Grief Recovery Handbook*, where I read that healing involves telling the entire story about the deceased instead of romanticizing or villainizing them, as we do when we only acknowledge the good or bad aspects of their personalities. Acknowledging the whole of our story helps us start moving past our grief. Until we can do that, the book counsels, we remain stuck.

This resonated deeply. For the past 21 years, I'd romanticized my father, discounting the deep psychological wounds he'd inflicted on me with his constant, cutting criticism. But those feelings were still there: the girl who'd started talking again after her father left, the pubescent who'd been repeatedly shamed over her changing body, the high schooler who'd been told there was no point in going to college because she was a girl—they were all still there, waiting to be let out. And they were pissed.

I brought all of my anger to my next session with Arielle. It was clear that I had to resolve all of this, but even just *thinking* about the emotional work this entailed made me livid. I'd already spent the past 21 years trying to resolve my issues with my father, and now I needed to do more? It wasn't fair that I had to do the tough emotional work of dealing with my parents' psychological baggage just because they hadn't.

And yet, I had no choice—not if I wanted to live a life that wasn't colored by the past. If I didn't want to do the work for myself, I knew that I would do it for my children. I simply couldn't bear to pass on this legacy of suffering to another generation.

So I got busy. I unpacked my anger and examined it. I acknowledged it, and I pushed against it to see what it was made of, discovering old, buried beliefs I'd inherited from my parents that I no longer supported. Beliefs like: the world is a cold place, and everyone's out to screw you. And: the only person you can trust is yourself.

Beneath that was sadness, a deep sorrow for the relationship that I'd always wanted with my father but had never been able to create. Once I could acknowledge the enormity of that loss, my anger began to recede.

The more I was willing to wade into the muck, the more easily it dissipated. Yes, that anger was part of my story and always had been. But now that I was finally acknowledging it, it no longer had a stranglehold on me.

As I was doing this work, I kept thinking of something shame and vulnerability researcher Brene Brown often says, that once you know your story, you get to write the ending.

Boy, was that true. For years, I'd minimized this critical part of my story. Now that I'd reclaimed it, I got to rewrite the ending. I no longer wanted my relationship with my father to be characterized by hurt and anger, just like I didn't want my *life* to be characterized by hurt and anger.

It was time to shore up a new narrative. To do that, I once again turned to books, starting with Rick Hanson's wonderful *Buddha's Brain: The Practical Neuroscience of Happiness, Love, and Wisdom*. Hanson's book gave me a foundational understanding of the brain science behind our actions, and taught me that we're hardwired to focus on negative events, especially those perceived as threats. This was a life-saving mechanism for our primitive brains, whose primary job was to help us survive.

Adrenaline, then, is the brain's chemical response to danger. If we're in danger, and about to be attacked by a lion, our brain releases adrenaline into our bodies, enabling us to fight that lion or else flee from it. The release of this adrenaline is known as the fight-flight mechanism.

Now here's the tricky part: adrenaline still courses through our body when we're in *perceived* danger, not just real danger. Meaning that even though most of us no longer face life-or-death situations in our daily lives, our adrenaline still kicks in during stressful moments like disagreements with our spouses or pressing work deadlines.

Furthermore, once that intense chemical cascade kicks in, we can't reason or think clearly; all we can do is run away, fight or freeze. And each time we respond in a certain way, we strengthen the particular neural pathways attached to that response, making it all the more likely that we'll respond to future threats in a similar fashion. Meaning that if I'm always yelling at the people who push my buttons, each new explosion keeps me that much more trapped in the cycle of yelling and fighting.

But Hanson's work was showing me another way. His research shows that we can *reprogram* our neural networks by choosing a new response. For example, we can choose peace instead of fighting, and we do this in a surprisingly simple way, by focusing on the experiences and feelings that we want to strengthen. In other words, by consciously choosing to focus on the good stuff in our lives, we strengthen the positive neural pathways in our brains. The inverse also holds true: focusing on the bad stuff strengthens the negative neural pathways in our brains. Keeping up this exercise over time—focusing on the feeling or response we want to create—is what ultimately rewires our brains.

So that's what I tried to do. When I had a positive interaction with Ken or the kids, I took 20-30 seconds to savor it, consciously imprinting the memory in my brain. Some days I remembered to do this exercise more than others, but I kept at it, and bit by bit, I began to see a difference. The more I focused on imprinting those positive family interactions on my brain, the more positive family experiences I began to experience.

For the next week, I kept Hanson's book by my bedside, re-reading key sections to help keep me on track. It was shocking to realize how deeply my brain was hardwired for negativity. "This negativity bias," Hanson says, "overlooks good news, highlights bad news and creates anxiety and pessimism."

When I read that passage, I felt as if someone had just unlocked a hidden room I hadn't known existed. My negative thoughts weren't because I was a weak or bad person. They were simply a biological function of survival.

That realization was breathtaking. Furthermore, "Your brain is like Velcro for negative experiences and Teflon for positive ones—even though most of your experiences are probably neutral or positive."

Those passages haunted me. What if my family story wasn't as negative as I'd always thought? What if there had been plenty of love and laughter in my childhood, but my brain simply hadn't been hardwired to remember them?

I found myself thinking about Nico and Gabriel's early years. For so long, I'd focused on the difficulty of that time. I loved my kids more than anything, but had found the adjustment to motherhood more difficult than most.

And yet, when I looked at photos from that period, they showed a different story. Instead of the stressed, harried new mother I expected to see, I found a peaceful and happy-looking new mother. How was it possible that I remembered so little of it?

My children's early childhood were gone, and I barely remembered the beauty of those days because my brain had been so focused on my exhaustion. And I could never, ever get that back.

That simple, little realization was devastating. What if the memories from my childhood had followed a similar trajectory? Perhaps my relationship with my father hadn't been singularly critical, as I recalled. Perhaps there had also been moments of love and connection, but I just didn't remember them.

For days, I mulled this over. Slowly but surely, I began to remember bits and pieces from my childhood: my father teaching me how to count to ten in French, my father teaching me how to juggle a soccer ball.

So I pulled out the old photos and took another look. This time around, I found evidence of a young, happy family. There we are on my third birthday, the four of us decked out in 70s finery; my mom with an arm around Marko, my father holding me as I stand on a wooden chair blowing out the candles of my cake, hands already smeared with chocolate.

And there we are, my father in long sideburns and a wide-lapel shirt, me in my brown dress with pink flowers, both of us wearing matching, shit-eating grins.

We looked *happy*, my father and I.

So what if it wasn't every day? That connection had existed once. And that love was what I now wanted to honor.

I wiped the dust off that old photo, popped it into a frame and set it on my bedroom dresser, where I'd see it every day. For the first time in years, my father was back in my home.

The next day was the 21st anniversary of my father's death, and I decided to mark it by inviting his spirit to join our family. Before dinner, Ken cracked a Beck's Dark and I opened up a bottle of red wine, my father's favorites. We poured the kids their special-occasion root beer, then we toasted my father. I lit a candle, said a short prayer and invited him into our family.

That was it, my small and simple ceremony. But it was enough. I could feel the changed energy in the room, and my heart felt much more free and accepting.

After dinner, I decided to frame one of my favorite photos of my parents—a faded print from the mid-60s, my mother sitting atop a stool as my father leans out behind her. My parents are facing the camera and smiling gently, looking more at ease than I remember in real life. I loved the contrast between them in this photo, my mother in a navy sweater and pedal pushers with made-up cat eyes, her jet-black hair coolly swirled into a beehive atop her head. My father stands behind her in a white oxford, his green eyes and fair coloring a pale contrast to my mother's olive-skinned complexion and darker hair.

It was one of my favorite photos of my parents, taken shortly after Marko had been born. My parents looked solid. They looked *happy*.

The kids loved it, too, and they had lots of questions like *That's Baba?!* and *Things look so different* and *Where's Uncle Marko?* After we'd fleshed out their questions, I placed the frame on our mantle, along with the rest of our family photos. My parents, welcome back into our lives.

Once we were past my father's anniversary, I felt a deep relief. I'd done it, survived both sets of holidays, this latest anniversary an exclamation point on the hard winter months I'd begun to think of as my season of grief.

Even though we were still in the thick of winter, I felt much more psychic space than I had since fall. Spring was coming. Light was coming. I didn't have to live in the muck anymore; I could move forward again. I *would* move forward.

With this came the urge to create an altar, a small space where I could go to light a candle, breathe. So I gathered a few of my favorite rocks and put them on my bedroom dresser, then added a stone my mother had given me. After that came a handful of childhood photos, plus the set of Buddhist prayer beads a friend had given me when Nico was little. Finally, a candle and a bag of sacred sand from a church in New Mexico that was said to having healing powers.

That was it. It was simple, and it was enough—a little space in the chaos, a place I could go to re-center, pray or remember my parents.

March. The days were starting to get longer and brighter, and we were all feeling the promise of spring. But since I was writing bits and pieces of the story that would one day become this book, I was still deeply involved in the grief process. The niggling feeling that I would work with grief in a larger way had begun to crystalize into the idea of teaching grief writing workshops. I wasn't yet sure what that would look like or how it would happen, so I just kept moving forward, hoping that the path would become eventually become clear.

At the same time, I realized that my own grief work wasn't quite complete. This I felt on a very deep level. So even though I didn't know what I needed to do next, I simply kept my eyes and ears open, following whatever path or book or experience felt right. Now that I had the gift of a few anniversary-free months before me, I felt a new lightness around my grief, a sort of freedom. I no longer *had* to do anything specific, and this, essentially, freed me up to do whatever I wanted.

This looser form of searching is what led me to Watsu, a passive form of bodywork based on Shiatsu and done in warm water. After reading an article by a woman who'd had a mystical, womb-like experience during her Watsu session, I scheduled an appointment for myself. It sounded a lot like what I'd been trying to achieve when I crawled into bed in the afternoons, nestling myself into a safe place.

Was this crazy? I wasn't sure as I drove to the appointment and nervously climbed into the water with Melanie, my Watsu practitioner. After Melanie strapped weights around my legs, she placed her arms around my back and began moving me through the water, stretching and cradling my body.

After a while, I became more comfortable in the water and time seemed to stretch out and disappear. At some point, I became aware of a distant rhythmic sound, like a heartbeat or muted drumming. Somehow, I knew I was back in my mother's womb. I floated here for a while, safe and loved and taken care of. A gentle swish of the water, and that disappeared. I was moving through the water again, held and supported, limbs gently stretching and retracting, completely and utterly relaxed. Here and there, I'd remember I was in the middle of a Watsu session before that, too, would float away. Time and space melded and refracted. Then, in just another passing moment, I became aware of God. And I became aware of my intense anger at God for abandoning me.

Tears leaked from my eyes, and the sharpness in my chest melted into deep sadness. I let the tears come as Melanie swished my body through the water, over and over again. After a while, that feeling melted away, and I'd become myself again, a middle-aged woman seeking solutions in a Watsu tank 30 minutes from her home.

By the end of our session, I was exhausted. On the drive home, I replayed the session in my mind. What a surprise it had been to feel that anger at God. To feel that I'd been *abandoned* by God.

I'd always thought of God as a more omnipresent type of spiritual presence, not any kind of localized presence who'd have a direct interest in me. But to have felt that level of abandonment assumed that we'd had a much more intimate relationship than I'd ever imagined. As intimate as a parent-child relationship, perhaps. Like a mother and daughter.

That shocked me. And if it was true, it meant that there was a lot more to this God/spiritual thing than I'd ever realized. As I drove home with these thoughts swirling about in my head, one thing became clear: I was no longer driving this story; the story was now driving *me*. And apparently spiritual rebirth was a big part of it.

A few days later, I chanced upon a book about near-death experiences. As I leafed through its pages, I found myself reading about people who feel angry with God for abandoning them as they transition from the spirit form into the physical body.

I know. *I know.*

Suffice it to say I was keeping my eyes and ears wide open as I continued about my daily life. Messages were coming fast and quick now, and I didn't want to miss them.

Meanwhile, the tattoo appointment I'd made the previous fall was quickly approaching. I found myself increasingly nervous as the day neared. What if I was making a mistake? I loved the traditional heart design I'd chosen, but something about the design felt off. By tattooing "MOM" in the middle of that heart, I feared I'd be stuck in my loss, endlessly repeating the story of my mother's death to anyone who asked. Instead of honoring my mother's death, I wanted to honor her life—a simple, little realization that showed me I'd turned another corner of my grief. But how?

The day before my appointment, Ken suggested I change the word "MOM" to "LOVE."

"That's more of what you're about, anyway," he said. "Just look at the 'Choose Love' bumper sticker you put on your car this winter."

That was true. "Choose love" was the lesson I kept trying to remember in challenging times. Choose love over fear. Choose love over anger. Choose love over having to be right. Choose love, choose love, *choose love.*

Everything I'd learned since my mother's death had taught me that love was never a mistake. Fear, almost always. So I bit the bullet and got the heart tattoo with the word "LOVE" in the middle. I left the tattoo parlor with my left shoulder bathed in new ink, smiling broadly.

Similar hints continued to arrive. I stumbled upon a Martha Beck article highlighting the importance of self-acceptance. "Self-acceptance frees you," she said, "self-rejection just makes you freeze."

Boy, was that true. Every time I negated some part of myself, life swirled out of control. When I found myself judging others, there was almost always some kind of self-judgment going on underneath. And the reverse was also true: the more I judged myself, the more critical I became of those around me.

When I caught myself in that downward spiral—snapping at Ken or the kids for some real or perceived injustice—I now took a time out and did a self-compassion exercise I'd learned from Kristin Neff's book, *Self-Compassion: The Proven Power of Being Kind to Yourself.*

What was it that I needed? I'd ask myself, hand on my heart. More often than not, it was the time and space to feel my feelings. Often, it was the realization that I needed to take care of myself by writing more consistently or going to my dance class. Sometimes I needed to get out of the house where I worked and mothered, to try something new, something fun. Other times, I just needed quiet.

These weren't new lessons, mind you, but they were arriving in a new way—wrapped in kindness and acceptance instead of self-judgment and fear. Neff's exercise in self-compassion was teaching me how to allow and accept whatever came up, without judging or trying to change it.

This small, seemingly insignificant practice—similar to what I'd learned at Kripalu—was a game changer. It was teaching me how to sit with my feelings and let them pass instead of clinging to them, as I'd done so often in the past. The more easily I could let those emotions move through me, the more quickly my life seemed to settle down, and the more quickly the people and events I'd viewed as challenges settled down as well.

During my next appointment with Arielle, I stumbled into an even deeper epiphany—that on a deep level, I still hadn't forgiven my parents for not being there for me emotionally when I was a child. This translated directly into other areas of my life. I let this realization seep in, light bulbs going off every which way I looked.

"Is this why I've been unable to forgive the friends who weren't there for me after my mother died?" I gasped.

Arielle nodded. "Exactly."

For days, I mulled this over. As a child, I'd been the one who took care of everyone else, never the person who asked for help. That pattern had continued into my adult life. I'd always been the person who noticed when something was awry, then worked to smooth it over, making sure everyone was all right. And I'd done that work willingly, at the expense of myself.

For so long, this was how I lived, waiting for others to see that I, too, needed love, help, attention, support. I'd simply assumed that others noticed my pain, picked up my non-verbal cues and emotions, as I did with others. But that wasn't how the world worked. And part of being a healthy adult, I was learning, was speaking up and asking for what I needed. Asking for help.

So why hadn't I done that earlier? Partly because I'd been so exhausted from trying to save everyone else, and partly because I didn't believe anyone would actually come to my aid if I needed it.

Because of this, I often did a strange push-pull dance in my relationships, remaining only half-in with the people I loved. When the going got tough, I distanced myself, pulling away emotionally. But if anything was ever going to change, the time was now.

So I started by reaching out to my friend, Becky, who was going through a messy divorce. Instead of simply trying to support her, as I'd done in the past, I stretched myself by telling her how much I missed my mom. And I admitted that I was still grappling with my loss.

When she responded with kindness and empathy, something within me opened, and I was finally able to talk about my mom for more than just a passing moment. It had been so long since I'd dared to really speak about my mother that I was shaking by the time I got off the phone.

Until that moment, I didn't realize how often I'd stopped myself from talking about my mother beyond the two or three people I thought could handle it. A part of me still felt ashamed that I wasn't over her death by now. But by not talking about my mother, I'd lost her twice.

Brene Brown's work on shame and resiliency provided me with the next piece of the roadmap; in particular, Brown's assertion that shame needs empathy to be healed. By trying to keep my shame over my lingering grief to myself, I was only making it worse. But when I could share that grief with Becky, who was able to listen without judging or trying to fix anything, my shame began to disappear.

It was a big lesson to have learned, and in the coming weeks, I reached out again and again to the friends who felt safe. The more vulnerable I allowed myself to be, the easier it was to reach out and ask for help. And each time one of those friends responded with kindness or empathy, I found myself bowled over with gratitude. Ken and Arielle weren't the only people who'd been there for me in my grief; others had been as well, I just hadn't asked.

For the next few weeks, I watched in fascination as a whole new world began to open up. For the first time in my life, I was starting to understand the value of community. Now that I was actually committed to my relationships, they were flowing much more smoothly. I no longer had the time or energy to worry about who was there for me and who wasn't because I was there for myself. And because I was there for myself, I was reaching out and asking for what I needed at every bend.

In doing so, I was rewiring the neural pathways in my brain, teaching myself that I wasn't alone and could trust others. That I could ascertain which friendships were ripe for deepening, steering away from those that weren't. And that I could trust myself throughout the process.

This wasn't any kind of overnight fix, mind you. I had to keep reminding myself to reach out and ask for help, that I could trust myself, as well as others. And I had to remember to savor those positive experiences with friends, imprinting them on my brain.

So I kept at it. Thinking in this new way was much like starting a new exercise routine or strengthening a muscle. But damn, it was worth it.

CHAPTER 15

WILD GEESE

I continued to actively look for new ways of doing things. With my 44th birthday around the corner, rituals kept coming to the fore. A good ritual, I knew, could help me contain my grief on my birthday, if not create a new family legacy. And yet, I was still struggling to find a birthday ritual that felt good enough, big enough, *right* enough.

Arielle and Scott, my grief counselor friend, helped me see that rituals didn't have to be big to be effective. They could be as simple as drinking coffee out of my mother's favorite coffee cup or celebrating an anniversary at my mother's favorite restaurant.

And I got to choose. For someone who'd been raised in a didactic and restrictive religion, it was incredibly freeing to realize I could choose the rituals that made the most sense for me. Furthermore, a ritual was something I could do just for myself. I didn't have to share it with anyone, nor did I have to get anyone's permission.

This rode squarely against my lifelong struggle to do things the *right* way—as if there's ever only one right way. That was part of the old story, and part of the self-criticism and perfectionism I'd inherited from my parents. Now that I had a larger toolbox, it was time to give that "not-enough" projection back to my parents. Once I did that, I could choose to connect to my parents in a new way, such as by retelling a childhood story or by writing my parents a letter and placing it in my memory box.

The way to do this was simply to practice it over and over again, as I'd learned in *Buddha's Brain*. When the urge to over-function, bypass my boundaries, save someone else or otherwise throw myself under the bus arose, that was my clue to step back and remind myself that I'd done enough. That *I was enough*, thereby reinforcing the new neural pathways I was building in my brain. In this way, bit by bit and day by day, I could create a new story.

Otherwise, I'd continue to remain trapped in the old story that I'd inherited from my parents. And while that family quest for perfectionism had kept me safe, it also kept me from living. In many ways, it had also kept me from loving. In a world where no one or nothing will ever be perfect, I could waste my entire life searching for that unattainable perfect thing. Essentially never leaving my house.

My perfectionism had also deeply affected my writing—the one area of my life where I had complete and absolute control. I could rewrite and rewrite until I was blue in the face, never sharing my writing with anyone until it was perfect.

Except that was no way to live. And it had kept me from sharing my gifts, not to mention bringing three previous books into the world. I was tired of living in constant fear, waiting for someone to call me out for not being perfect. I wasn't perfect and never would be. But I *was* good enough.

Being "good enough," then, became my new mantra. When I cooked dinner, I chose a simple, easy-to-prepare meal and let that be enough. When friends came over, I let a 15-minute emergency house clean be enough. When I bought a gift for a friend, I no longer stymied myself by searching for that one perfect gift, but chose one or two things I thought she'd like. Good enough.

There was so much freedom in this new way of living that it quickly became addictive. I became a master at the 20-minute, first-floor house clean. Good enough to get us through the week. Three dinners planned for the week? Youbetcha. Twenty-five minutes to hit the neighborhood grocery store to pick up that food? Awesome. Dropping off take-out from a friend's favorite restaurant when her family needed extra support and Ken and I were so slammed with work that we could barely cook for our own family? Damn straight. Clearly defining the amount of time I could realistically volunteer at my children's school? Fuck yeah.

Now that I had more time and distance from my mother's death, I was starting to realize how easy it would be to keep hiding in my grief. I'd needed all the extra time and space I'd given myself during that first year, and in many ways my introverted self still did. But I was also starting to see that, if I wasn't careful, that time and space could become another type of prison, a way of isolating and keeping myself safe. I could essentially hide in my grief forever.

That was why I kept challenging myself, taking baby steps when I wasn't ready for leaps. Reaching out to a friend I wanted to get to know better. Meeting a close friend for dinner instead of a larger, more unwieldy group. Publishing a few essays on the topic of grief before publishing an entire book.

Step by step, day by day. Remembering to breathe when the anxiety kicked in, that none of this had to be perfect. Focusing on this moment, *right here, right now*. Feeling the air on my skin, the sun on my face. Breathing in, breathing out. One moment at a time.

And I applied my new "good enough" attitude to the concept of forgiveness. For so long, I'd felt that there had to be some trick to forgiving my parents and for forgiving the past. But what I was learning is that forgiveness comes in bits and pieces. As we feel the old feelings, we're able to release them.

It's a process, then. There's no magical wand, as I'd hoped, just the ebb and flow of life as we move two steps forward, then one back. The real trick happens as we learn to forgive ourselves.

In the end, I got my birthday wish. It didn't happen as I was expecting, wasn't centered around some big, beautiful ritual I'd magically created. Nope. Like the rest of life, it was messy and imperfect.

My feelings of inadequacy had increased as my birthday approached, and in an attempt to find some peace of mind, I'd gone to see Arielle. I no longer saw her regularly, as I had after my mother's death, instead going back when I needed extra support, as I did with my birthday. I was feeling angry, unmoored, unhappy with everything and everyone around me. In short, my inner critic was having a field day. Life sucked, and I sucked with it.

So I brought all that to Arielle. As I worked my way through it in her office, she helped me see that my parents' burden had never been mine to carry, and it was time to give that back.

So, right then and there, we did a little ceremony. She encouraged me to envision my parents sitting in the empty seats before me. Then I did a visualization in which I handed my parents' suffering and feelings of failure back to them. After they'd taken all of that back, Arielle asked me to choose how I wanted to connect to my parents.

I thought about this for a few moments. What if I could connect to my parents through love instead? What if I could connect to them through joy and possibility? *Success* instead of failure. What if I could connect to my parents by releasing the burdens of the past?

There was so much possibility in this new story that tears were soon streaming down my face. Then the craziest thing happened. My father, who'd been in my mind's eye the whole time, smiled his 900-kilowatt smile and said, "I'm so glad, *zlato*. We've been waiting for this."

I was shaking by this point, half-sobbing and half-laughing. My parents had been *waiting* for me to bust through the old chains, to finally choose love over fear, be happy?

Goddamn.

This whole time, had it really been that easy? What it came down to, all along, was simply making a choice.

Over the next few weeks, I found myself applying the lesson of choice and happiness to my relationships with Ken and the kids. For so long, I'd done a similar push-pull dance with them— distancing when I needed space, then arguing in an attempt to get close. It was another pattern that I was ready to break. As with my parents, I no longer wanted to connect to my husband and children through strife and discord. Instead, I wanted harmony. I wanted peace.

To admit this to myself was at once shocking and healing. For so long, I'd been proud of my defiance. It was a trait that had defined who I was and how I functioned in the world. But that defiance had also kept me separate. And I was tired of living a lonely existence, separated from the people I most loved.

Acknowledgment that I was on the right path came in bits and pieces, whispers then shouts. One day, I noticed that The Death Routine no longer triggered me. I still felt a twinge at the opening song, but there were no more tears. Wyclef Jean's song about death was just another reminder of how far I'd come. Yes, I still wished my mother was alive. But I couldn't go back to the life I'd led then. Her death had shocked me awake, become the catalyst I hadn't known I needed.

While attending a grief workshop one Saturday afternoon, I found myself wrestling with the feeling that I didn't want to be there. Everything about the workshop resonated, but I couldn't shake the feeling that I was ready to move on. Ironically, the workshop was the type of event I'd ached for after my mother's death. At the time, I hadn't been able to find what I needed. Now, these events were popping out of the woodwork. In the span of two weeks, I'd fielded four invitations to events around the topic of death.

I'd attended the grief workshop because I felt like I should. It would bolster my research, I reasoned, not to mention my own journey. But that wasn't what I wanted, and my body let me know it. Over and over again during the workshop, it asked for sunshine. Over and over again, it asked for freedom. All the while, the opening lines from Mary Oliver's poem "Wild Geese" ran through my head:

> *You do not have to be good.*
> *You do not have to walk on your knees*
> *for a hundred miles through the desert repenting.*
> *You only have to let the soft animal of your body*
> *love what it loves.*

I left the workshop early, walking out into the clear blue afternoon as the seminar doors slammed shut behind me. My body wanted sunshine and laughter. It wanted to play. So I let it.

Amen.

EPILOGUE

Anything is possible. Stay open forever, so open it hurts, and then open up some more, until the day you die, world without end, amen.

—GEORGE SAUNDERS,
THE BRAINDEAD MEGAPHONE

After Isabel Allende's daughter died, Allende's mother told her nothing could fix or alleviate her sorrow. But if she continued to move forward, one step at a time, there would eventually be light at the end of a long, dark tunnel.

It's been three years since my mother died and one of my biggest lessons is that there is no happy ending. There's no turning back the clock, no magical potion to soothe the pain.

What there *is* is a choice. The choice to move forward again, one step at a time, regardless of what happens tomorrow. The choice to keep our hearts open instead of shutting down from the pain. To learn how to hold them both in the palms of our hands, the joy alongside the sorrow.

I believe grief takes tremendous courage. It asks us to climb into the fire when it feels as if it might burn us alive. It asks us to stay true to ourselves when the world around us encourages anything but.

People who are grieving, I've come to understand, are often seen as a threat—a clear reminder that the world we've created may not be as safe as it seems; that one day, we'll all lose a loved one.

When someone runs from you in their grief, it's almost always because of their demons. Hold on to those who stay. They're your champions.

When my kids were young, I couldn't understand why our house was such a disaster. No matter how many times I picked up, the clutter seemed to spawn overnight. Back then, I thought I could do it once and have it be done.

There is no "done," I've come to understand. Not when the nature of life is change. Nothing ever stays the same, much as we might want it to. The house accumulates clutter much as our lives accumulate days, weeks and hours. Children stretch and grow before our very eyes. Trees blossom; flowers die. Each season becomes another transition; another opportunity to check in, notice the curve and wind of our path. Each ending, a new beginning.

Writing this book has enabled me to chart my way forward, carve out my own living prayer. I continue that prayer each time I choose to recommit to harmony instead of strife, each time I take a deep breath before snapping at my loved ones, each time I step outside to reground myself.

When I find myself acting in the old, critical ways, I recognize them as a red flag, another chance to course-correct. How *else* can I connect with my loved ones? How *else* can I connect with my parents? I'm older, now, and a bit wiser; I can connect through love and laughter. Through gratitude. Presence. And I can always, always connect through love.

I'm still peeling the onion, still uncovering new layers to my grief, still finding new ways forward. Part of what I've discovered is my tendency to use grief as a security blanket in times of fear, hiding behind it instead of stretching myself.

Like my old perfectionist tendencies, fear keeps me safe. It keeps me from having to put myself out in the world. Except that's no longer how I want to live.

More often than not, I can move through my fear just by acknowledging it. It's almost always less scary to move through it than it is to run from it. And if I'm really caught in the crossfire, I do a gratitude meditation that I learned at Kripalu. When I'm unable to climb out on my own, gratitude always helps.

I used to hate it when people would tell me to trust the process of grief. I didn't *want* to trust the process. I wanted a quick fix to my grief. Essentially, I wanted my loss to go away, for my mother's death to have never happened.

Part of grief's function, I've learned, is to teach me acceptance. Acceptance of the past, of the present moment, of where I am today.

Learning to trust myself has been an essential part of this process. To trust my anger, my rage, my joy, my love, my laughter—each one has played a role in my healing process.

One of the hardest things I've had to do was allow them to show me their wisdom. Often, that meant getting out of my own way.

Permission has been just as crucial. Giving myself the permission I need instead of waiting for someone else to do it. Permission to make my own rules, and then the permission to change them.

Renegotiating, reorienting each and every day.

As my son Nico once said, "The good thing about the future is that you can always change it."

After the second anniversary of my mother's death, I found myself dreading another big *Slava* celebration. I'd been sick for weeks, and the idea of hosting a giant party as I was fighting off a lingering illness was just too much.

So I let myself off the hook, deciding to take care of myself instead. At a grief retreat with Sobonfu Some a few months prior, she'd encouraged us to ask our ancestors for help—put them to work, she advised, just like you do any houseguest who stays for more than a couple of days.

So I sat down and wrote my ancestors a letter, explaining I wouldn't be able to host a fancy *Slava* celebration this year. Instead of automatically following the old rituals, I would now consciously weigh each ritual to determine whether it would help my family or hinder it. Then I would choose accordingly.

Furthermore, I asked my ancestors to help me create a new family legacy based on harmony instead of strife. It wasn't anything personal, I wrote, it was simply what I needed to do for myself and my family. I hoped they understood. I simply couldn't honor them in the old, unconscious ways any longer. I signed the letter with love before adding it to my memory box.

Right before my mother's birthday, I dreamt she was dying again. But this time, she was dying at home, without the chemo, without the hospital and without the doctors.

We were in a nondescript, cozy room, and my mother was conscious and comfortable. Once again, I had to go through the awful heartbreak of saying goodbye to her. But our goodbye was slower this time, more peaceful, and my mother was even able to give me a loving hug.

In my dream, I sat with her as her breaths became slower and slower, tears streaming down my face. I didn't need to fight anything. All I had to do was hold on.

As the third anniversary of my mother's death approached, I realized I was ready to bring excitement back into my life. After having emerged from my cocoon, it was time to move to the next level and explore the limits of what was possible. What *else* did I want for my life?

Most of us don't think of excitement as one of life's primary building blocks, and for a long time, I didn't, either. But what I learned is that when we don't have excitement in our lives, we self-sabotage in order to create it. Meaning we drink, shop, argue, gossip, gamble, have affairs or spend endless hours online in an attempt to feel alive, to feel our hearts beat faster.

My wake-up call arrived in a different fashion. As I was struggling with a draft of this book, my 28-year-old second cousin from Serbia—who I'd met once—came to visit us for three months. Fenced in by a crumbling Serbian economy, Vlado had come to the U.S. seeking other possibilities.

Our household of boys expanded to include one more, and the dynamic in our house changed dramatically. Nico and Gabriel were ecstatic to have a six-foot, two-inch cousin on the premises, and my soccer-loving kids spent hours chasing Vlado around, questioning him about his semi-pro soccer goalie past.

Meanwhile, we adults had numerous conversations around Vlado's next steps. He could work this job or that, follow the thread of his previous career, go back to school, explore a new relationship or move to a new country. These were all possibilities that Ken and I had abandoned since having children, and simply being around that energy of possibility was invigorating.

I found myself thinking about the person I'd been at 28: fresh from my years of tending bar, about to start graduate school and follow my dream of becoming a writer, free and open in a way I wasn't now.

And then I'd shut it all down. Become the serious, studious person I thought I needed to be to survive graduate school.

Yes, I'd been a bit of a hellion at age 28. But I'd also enjoyed life. I'd laughed a lot, had awesome friends and was willing to try new things. I was willing to *risk.*

Where had all that gone?

I ached for another taste of that possibility, that freedom. And I didn't want it in the way that society encourages at midlife, by buying a nicer car, taking fancy vacations or drinking copious amounts of alcohol. Since having children, drinking seemed to be the most socially accepted way parents created space in their lives, how we created freedom.

Except that I was tired of that kind of "freedom," particularly after having spent my 20s partying and tending bar. I wanted true freedom, the kind of excitement that doesn't come in a bottle, and a life that's built around *possibility* instead of lack.

So I backed off the wine and I backed off the complaining. I consciously thought about the words that were leaving my lips, and tried to surround myself with others who did the same. And I fanned the excitement I'd felt when I first started writing this book.

After three years of chipping away on my grief memoir, it was time to finish my book. If there was ever a time to put my new "good enough" philosophy into action, this was it. So I got off the perfectionist high-horse that had kept me writing and revising, endlessly polishing and tearing apart words and passages, and got to work. It was time to move on from the story of grief in which I'd been living for the past few years and I knew it. Vlado's appearance in my life had only cemented that knowledge.

I had other work to do in the world, and spending 10 years writing a grief memoir wasn't going to get me there. I was ready to teach workshops again, help people harness the power of their stories through the magic of writing. None of which could be accomplished if I were still sitting at my desk working on the same book for the next decade, pulling the world in at its seams, refusing to let anyone or anything in.

As I worked on completing my "good enough" book, I also began to reconnect with the joyful, free-spirited 28-year-old who still lived inside of me. She may have been reckless at times, but she also knew how to live, and my 45-year-old self needed those reminders.

So I bought myself a kick-ass pair of cowboy boots and went out dancing. I began to connect with friends on a deeper, more meaningful level, and I carved out time to reconnect with Ken, as well as opened an ongoing conversation about the importance of bringing a sense of adventure back into our little family.

And I started saying YES more instead of my default NO. I learned how to snowboard, and I loved it. I started writing poetry again, asked Gabriel to teach me how to throw a fastball and did my best to keep up with Nico as he dove into Parkour. I took an investing class, then started a business mastermind group with a powerful set of women. When things got dicey, I clearly advocated for myself and my loved ones.

And I stopped hiding in my bedroom when things felt too big or scary. Yes, I still took time and space for myself—that would always remain an important way for my introverted self to recharge—but I no longer *hid* there. I did my best to dwell in possibility instead.

These days, I think a lot about intentions. What do I want my day to be like? What do I want my *life* to be like? This simple little exercise is teaching me how to corral my mind. It's also teaching me how to bring compassion into the cracks and crevices of my life. Kindness and fun. Ease and joy. Presence.

I've learned that it's up to me to set the stage not only for what kind of life I want to live but also for what kind of day I'm having. Instead of reacting to everything that comes my way, I'm learning to be proactive. To create the joy I want to feel. To create that connection.

And I continue to refine my own set of rituals. I'll often drink my coffee out of my mother's favorite mug when I miss her. I light lots of candles. And I continue to tell stories about her because she continues to be part of my life.

Community remains key in my healing process. I recently read that loneliness activates the same parts of the brain as physical pain. *The same parts.* Imagine how much more painful that becomes during times of grief.

I continue to grow my personal community, and have started leading my own grief writing workshops. Community remains a key element of those workshops, whether they're in person or online. To see the shift that occurs when someone's grief is acknowledged in community is astonishing, nothing short of magic.

Finally, I choose to believe that my mother's spirit remains near. I no longer see hawks as frequently as I once did, but they often appear when I most need them. Like the week before my dog Loki died, when I'd found myself burdened by an ominous sadness I couldn't shake. At the time, Loki was about to turn 12, slowing down but otherwise seemingly healthy. As I often did, I'd taken Loki with me on multiple walks, trying to shake my sadness. We saw three different hawks that week, each flying low, as if to make sure we didn't miss them.

That weekend, a few hours before I was to take Loki in for a regularly scheduled vet visit, I found him hiding in the backyard in pain, unable to walk. Later that night, as he was getting prepped for back surgery, we learned that Loki had zero platelets and wouldn't survive surgery. He had an autoimmune disease that comes on quickly, the vet told us, with no symptoms. Meaning there was nothing we could do. Nothing except wake our boys and bring them to the vet at 10:30 p.m. on a Friday night so we could say goodbye to our beloved pup. The most accepting and loving companion I'd ever known.

Shortly after Loki's sudden death, I completed the final chapter of this book. I was feeling a deep sense of loss, as I often do with endings. Saying goodbye to my beloved dog had been hard enough, and now I was also saying goodbye to the project that had kept me connected me to my mother.

I slept fitfully that night, caught in a web of dreams, unable to find my mother. When I awoke, I felt unsettled. As I moved through the mechanics of our morning, getting the kids breakfast, taking them to school, I kept catching whiffs of my mother's perfume.

I continued through the day with a heavy heart. At one point, I found myself drawn to a Rosamunde Pilcher book on my bookshelf, *September*, that Marko had given me as he was clearing out the final batch of my mother's things. After I'd taken the book home, I'd forgotten about it. Now it was staring me in the face. What did it want?

I shook my head and got back to work. A few hours later, after revising a draft of my final chapter, I went for a walk around Wonderland Lake, close to our home. It was a chilly March day, and I pulled my too-thin coat close as I picked up my pace. There, waiting for me atop a barren tree at the start of the path, was a giant hawk. I walked up to the tree in awe, pulled out my phone and took a few photos.

Nothing. The hawk didn't move, not even when I was directly under it. I took another photo, then stopped for a moment of reverence. It waited until I'd walked away, then flew past me, nearly buzzing me.

When I got home, I pulled out my journal and revisited the previous night's dreams, trying to decipher their meaning. As I was writing, a Rosamunde Pilcher passage a friend had recently sent me popped into my head. On a hunch, I pulled the book *September* off my bookshelf and started leafing through it. There it was, toward the end.

> *Death is nothing at all. It does not count. I have only slipped away into the next room. Nothing has happened. Everything remains exactly as it was. I am I, and you are you, and the old life that we lived so fondly together is untouched, unchanged. Whatever we were to each other, that we are still. Call me by the old familiar name. Speak of me in the easy way which you always used. Put no difference into your tone. Wear no forced air of solemnity or sorrow. Laugh as we always laughed at the little jokes that we enjoyed together. Play, smile, think of me, pray for me. Let my name be ever the household word that it always was. Let it be spoken without an effort, without the ghost of a shadow upon it. Life means all that it ever meant. It is the same as it ever was. There is absolute and unbroken continuity. What is this death but a negligible accident? Why should I be out of mind because I am out of sight? I am but waiting for you, for an interval, somewhere very near, just round the corner. All is well.*

I closed the book, tears in my eyes. Perhaps I hadn't imagined my mother's perfume that morning after all. Nor had I imagined the significance of the hawk. Perhaps I hadn't imagined *any of it*. Maybe, just maybe, my mother had been sending me messages all along.

Thank God I'd been paying attention.

ACKNOWLEDGMENTS

I once heard Ann Patchett say that writing about her deceased friend Lucy Grealy was like holding her hand to a hot stove and seeing how long she could keep it there. At times, this book was my stove. Incredible, loving thanks to Ken for his love and support throughout it all. I'm so grateful for his presence in my life.

So much grace to my children, Nico and Gabriel. I'm blessed beyond belief to be your mother. Thank you for your love, your light, your laughter and your joy, as well as for simply being who you are.

There were so many levels of healing that needed to happen for me to write this book, and central to that was Arielle Schwartz's unconditional care and support. Joyful, kick-ass thanks also go to Juliet Seskind and the entire Ayre community. Thank you all.

Loving, gracious, multi-faceted thanks to Liz Rodriguez, Becky Schulteis Veenstra, Jess Jaret, Sherrie Scott, Sandra Trbović, Sarah Boyd, Mads Pollak, Eileen Kiernan-Johnson, Rachel Manzo, Chip Frye, Larry Bloskas, Michelle Maloy Dillon, Perrin Chipouras, Jennifer Hinton, Dana Stillman, Alexa Allen, Jean Anthony, Emily O'Brien, Michael Murphy, Mo

Breed, Dana Runge, Ann Harris, Steve Parrish, Sara Wright, Kathleen Love and Ivana Momić Vitanovska.

Dean. Kick-ass, loving thanks for your love, support and sharp hilarity, as well as for all the years of web help and support. Loving thanks to Jules and Milena, too.

Vladimir Gavrančić for stirring the pot. When you coming back, 'cuz?

Giant hugs to Carissa Travis, Ashley Smith and Samuel LaCasse for loving, adventurous and joyful child care that meant more than you'll ever know. Thanks also to my children's wonderful teachers, especially Jessie Vanden Hogen and Holly Vance.

Michelle Maloy Dillon for her beautiful author photos, as well as for helping me co-create and co-facilitate that first, magical "Reclaiming Yourself After Loss" workshop.

Thomas McGee at Rightly Designed for his gorgeous book cover.

Hynek Palatin for his interior design wizardry.

Barb Colombo at 11:11 Productions for her essential, mystical photos.

A special shout-out to soul sister Sandra Trbović for providing critical book support along the way. Another round of loving thanks to my dear friends Jess Jaret and Sarah Boyd for their help with the manuscript. Thanks also to Carol Monhollen and John DuGene for manuscript feedback and support.

Deep thanks to Becky and Steve Hardesty for allowing me to use their beautiful home as a writing space at a critical juncture. Thanks also to Wendy Clough and Josh Lipton for opening their mountain retreat to me during an earlier impasse.

An early thanks to Kiese Laymon for championing my piece at *Gawker*, showing me that there was an audience for my grief story.

This is a book of becoming. Becoming one person, then another. As such I'd like to extend my gratitude to the Madison friends who were there for me after my father's death, especially Becky, Liz, Jody, Shanta and Joman, as well as the folks at the Irish and the Crystal. Lord, that's another book entirely.

Deep gratitude to those who supported my professional path during this period, particularly Jesse Lee Kercheval, Toma Longinović, Nancy Reisman and Ron Kuka at the University of Wisconsin-Madison, as well as Tony Ardizzone, Alyce Miller, Andrew Shea, Henry R. Cooper, Jr. and my fellow writers at Indiana University. Thanks, too, to Betsy Draine at UW-Madison for introducing me to Zora Neale Hurston's *Their Eyes Were Watching God* and Louise Erdrich's *Love Medicine*, forever altering my path as a writer.

Grateful thanks to the International Institute of Education and the wonderful Fulbright program, as well as to the late Aleš Debeljak for his support during my year in Slovenia.

Another essential round of thanks to the late Jake Adam York for his support at the University of Colorado-Denver.

A deep bow of gratitude to the following (incomplete) list of writers, teachers and movers and shakers whose work has helped me on this particular journey: Brene Brown, David Harshada Wagner, David Kessler, Kristin Neff, Elisabeth Kübler-Ross, Rick Hanson, Trevor Blake and the fantastic TSS community, Michael Franti & Spearhead, Anita Moorjani, Tom Shadyac, Sobonfu Some, Meghan O'Rourke, Sue Frederick, Jen Louden, Susannah Conway, Jo Klima, Briana and Peter Borten, Christine Kane, Liz Gilbert, Glennon Doyle Melton, Tara Mohr, Martha Beck, Amy Cuddy and Mary Oliver.

Last not but not least, I would like to thank *you*. This book becomes something else entirely in your hands, a transmission between our hearts, hopes and dreams. From the bottom of my heart, thank you. *Namaste.*

REFERENCES

Brown, Brene. *Daring Greatly: How the Courage to Be Vulnerable Transforms the Way We Live, Love, Parent, and Lead.* New York, NY: Avery, 2012.

Brown, Brene. *Rising Strong: The Reckoning. The Rumble. The Revolution.* New York, NY: Spiegel & Grau, 2015.

Hanson, Rick, Ph.D., and Richard Mendius, M.D. *Buddha's Brain: The Practical Neuroscience of Happiness, Love, and Wisdom.* Oakland, CA: New Harbinger Publications, 2009.

Kübler-Ross, Elisabeth and David Kessler. *Life Lessons: Two Experts on Death and Dying Teach Us About the Mysteries of Life and Living.* New York, NY: Scribner, 2003.

Levy, Alexander. *The Orphaned Adult: Understanding and Coping with Grief and Change After the Death of Our Parents.* Boston, MA: Da Capo Press, 2000.

Neff, Kristin, Ph.D. *Self-Compassion: The Proven Power of Being Kind to Yourself.* New York: Harper Collins, 2011.

Pilcher, Rosamunde. *September.* New York, NY: St. Martin's Press, 1991.

Ware, Bronnie. *The Top Five Regrets of the Dying: A Life Transformed by the Dearly Departed.* Carlsbad CA: Hay House, Inc., 2012.

ABOUT THE AUTHOR

Tanja Pajevic received her M.F.A. from Indiana University and has taught at the University of Colorado Denver, the Community College of Denver and Indiana University, as well as in the larger community. She is the author of *9 Steps to Heal Your Resentment and Reboot Your Marriage*, a self-help book based on her blog *Reboot This Marriage: Two adults. Two kids. One year to reboot this marriage.* Her writing has appeared in *The New York Times, Huffington Post, Gawker* and *Scary Mommy*, as well as in literary magazines.

Tanja is the recipient of a Fulbright grant, Hemingway Fellowship, Kraft Fellowship and a faculty award from the University of Colorado Denver for her project "Writing as Healing." Inspired by the challenges we all face but rarely discuss, Tanja leads writing workshops around life's big transitions. She lives in Boulder, CO, with her husband Ken and their two boys, Nico and Gabriel, and is currently completing a book of poetry.

Connect with her and find out more about her workshops at TanjaPajevic.com.

Made in the USA
Coppell, TX
13 May 2020